My Blind Dog *Still* Wags His Tail

Missy,
Enjoy the book.
Be Encouraged!
Jill

My Blind Dog *Still* Wags His Tail

Uplifting Life Lessons From My Best Friend

J. D. Wilcock

Illustrations by Brittany Johnson

My Blind Dog *Still* Wags His Tail

ISBN-13: 978-1535176927
ISBN-10: 153517692X

Book Production by Bard Design
alanbard@alanbard.com

Illustrations by Brittany Johnson
bwilco2@icloud.com

Author: J.D. Wilcock
jd@jdwilcock.com

PO Box 447
Ozark, MO 65721

Dedicated to

My wonderful son, Jay, who is the true apple of my eye. I am grateful we shared the love and joy of our beloved best friend Hushie.

In Memory of

Kenneth McNab Wilcock

Acknowledgements

I never realized all the people and behind the scenes pieces it would take to complete this book. I am grateful for the original idea and vision. I would have to attribute that to God and my dog Hushie. I hope that is not the first time God and a dog have been given near equal credit! This vision and idea was born deep in my soul and carried me though the lulls in the project.

I want to thank my wife Denise for supporting all the time invested in this work. She was intimately involved with the stories and helped clarify them along the way. She also provided the interior book photos. Thank you to my son Jay. He was always supportive and understanding. There were times I was holed up in my office for quite a few Saturdays. I never heard him complain. He also took the awesome cover photo.

I am an idea person and a communicator, these are things I do well. So I want thank the following people for tackling the tasks that don't come easy for me. Thanks to my brother Paul. He is one of a few people on earth who can decipher my handwriting. Pretty much because his looks similar. He took my original handwritten drafts and put them in a legible word document. No small task and at the time I thought 'now we are getting somewhere'. Thank you to my cousin Susan Geren. She helped with some original editing. We had some great times, good laughs and occasional challenges working through the original work. I found it helpful to sit with her at the dining room table reading out loud the original manuscript. She is the first who said this is going to take more than a few weeks or months. Months bah humbug. Two years later I saw she was right.

I want to thank my first writers group. From that came my three original key proof readers for the whole book. Thank you Nora, Brenda and Susanna. Thanks to our family friend Sophonia and her excellent and further fine-tuned editing. After all these were complete it took a good three months to sort through the changes. Fortunately, the original vision remained intact.

Thank you to my second and current writers group in humble Pierce City Mo. We have an actual multi published author in our midst, Polly McCrillis. She offered great insight at the meetings. She and others were available other times to answer my plethora of questions. Thank you to all the writers and characters in this unique group.

Thank you to the Lakeside, Ohio writer's workshop for insights into book publishing. Thank you to my nephew and niece Evander and Adia Wilcock. Although children they are advanced readers. They tackled the book even though it has some disturbing events. Since it is our family history the parents, Richie and Amber, agreed it would be ok. The young and voracious readers gave me a big thumbs up on the book. I have to believe it was from their heart. Thank you Richie just in case a little coaching to encourage was re-quired. Whatever the case I was lifted up by their response.

I want to thank my illustrator Brittany Johnson. Despite the responsibility of being a new mom she jumped in with both feet to translate my vision in a graphic way. She does excellent work and is a gifted artist. Go to the books Facebook page to see her renditions in vibrant full color. Thanks to Garret, her husband, for letting us hand off Orla to you a little more than normal during this process.

Thank you to Rick and Debra Tucker for sage simple advice. She is a published author and he does illustrative work, including the front cover header. They offered some key insightful recommendations. Thank you to Tim Vonbecker, creative fine artist, and ad man, who helped with ideas about the front cover. These three friends are all part of my wonderful and supportive church Life Group.

Thank you to Barb Caffrey. Recommended by Polly McCrillis to do a final copy edit. I appreciate your encouragement and expertise. We worked closely for six months. I learned a tremendous amount from you. Also thank you to Alan Bard for your help with formatting for e-readers and the paper bound copy. He worked tirelessly formatting all the disparate images and photos.

Finally, thanks to each of you. Whether you are a reader or a friend or acquaintance along the way, ultimately these stories and lessons are meant for you to enjoy and ponder.

Table of Contents

Chapter 1	Left for Dead	15
Chapter 2	Uniquely You	33
Chapter 3	Simplify	45
Chapter 4	Survive or Thrive	61
Chapter 5	Full of Grace	71
Chapter 6	Let's Just Get Along	83
Chapter 7	Today Is My Last Day	97
Final Thoughts		105
Author's Afterword		107

Appendix

- No Kill Animal Shelters 113
- Service Dog Agencies 117
- Interesting Dog Facts 123
- Quotes About Dogs 125
- Inspirational Links 131
- Resources to Discover Gifts and Talents 133

My Blind Dog *Still* Wags His Tail

Chapter 1

Left for Dead

It was a normal, lazy Sunday night, one of those evenings that reminds everyone why that day is a favorite time for rest and reflection. Everything was right with the world. The lawn looked wonderful as the final shadows fell across the landscape. The grill had cooled, but a slight aroma of barbecued chicken and vegetables wafted up to the deck. Later that night, a clear sky and full moon would illuminate a wonderful tapestry of stars. All the chores were done. Dinner had been served and eaten. I had a plan for Monday and the week was all set. It was time to relax.

Then, in an instant, everything changed.

In the late evening, we noticed that our six-year-old beagle mix, Hushie, couldn't walk. Dazed and unresponsive, he stumbled as he tried to push off his back legs. His tongue sagged out of his mouth like a man taking his last gasps of life in the desert. He had been fine all day and had never exhibited symptoms or behavior like this.

We were nervous and frustrated. He did not react to our gentle touches or voices. Hushie usually was lively and vibrant, and responded well to us. Now there was nothing but a blank, lifeless stare in his eyes.

We watched and waited, but after an hour, there was no improvement. Should we wait until morning to take him to our vet, or should we take him to the emergency vet clinic now?

My wife Denise was unable to watch as I gathered up our beloved pet and placed him in our vehicle. His body was limp, and his breathing was shallow. He could not even open his eyes. Was our dear Hushie even going to make it to the vet, much less through the night?

Adrenaline turned fear into action. My brain switched to an automatic mode, a sort of "we just have to get this done" mentality.

It was close to midnight and the only veterinarian was fifteen miles away. With Hushie in the backseat of our SUV, I headed for the emergency veterinary clinic. I listened for his faint breathing to make sure he hung on. The roads were clear and barren, with not a soul in sight. Springfield is a small city and we weren't sure if an actual vet would be there. We called, but only got voice mail, yet they said they were open 24/7. Fortunately, when we arrived there was a vet at the clinic.

After examining Hushie for an hour, the emergency vet was perplexed. She advised me to take him home, keep him calm, and spoon-feed him water through the night. She told us to take him to our regular vet in the morning.

Needless to say, it was a long and uncomfortable night.

We took turns and sat on the floor just to be near Hushie. We softly stroked him to give a familiar touch, just as a mother would for her sick child. After all, he had become a cherished member of our tribe. Hushie remained unchanged throughout that night. He was paralyzed and catatonic.

We spent a sleepless night full of uncertainty. For the first time, we faced the real possibility that we could lose him to some mysterious illness.

On Monday morning at first light, we went to our own vet, who knew Hushie well. We hoped he would have some answers for us.

Our vet ran a battery of tests and asked that Hushie stay overnight. He was set up in a private area. Although it was a spartan cage, we were able to provide a blanket that might remind him of our scent. We had been opening his mouth and dribbling the water in to make sure he stayed hydrated. He would not even lap water with his tongue; it was as if he was comatose. Now an IV was inserted into his boney leg to provide fluids since he could not drink.

We spent another restless night grappling with the unknown. We made lots of calls to other vet clinics. We researched the Internet about what could cause these bizarre symptoms. But we were still clueless as to what was going on.

Denise went in the next morning, Tuesday, to see Hushie. He was lying still in the sterile room, all by himself. It had now been two long days with no real change. The vet warned Denise that Hushie had remained unresponsive. Yet when Denise entered the room, Hushie opened his eyes, albeit only for a brief moment. He looked at her and wagged his tail once, then he closed his eyes and continued to lie still.

Denise and the vet staff were amazed. As he clung to life, Hushie was still able to provide this faint response, even to wagging his beloved, distinctive tail. Denise had to get back to work, so we left our pup with the vet for one more day to receive 'round the clock care'.

On Wednesday, our vet informed us that Hushie hadn't improved overnight. There was only that one little flicker of hope the previous day when he'd wagged his tail. I will never forget the vet's simple, clear words: "There is nothing more I can do for him, but I could put him down for you." It came across in a matter-of-fact, businesslike tone.

I felt my body seize and tense up in shock and confusion. I thought, *This is all too fast! This is my cherished friend, playmate, and companion! How can we end his life without giving him a chance to recover?* After all, it was only a week earlier that Hushie had bounded all over the yard, chased his ball, and ate like a horse! Had we investigated every option?

Denise's maternal instincts kicked in. She determined that we had to keep him under her wing at least another day or two. In less than two minutes, Denise and I agreed that we needed more time. There were just too many unknowns. We told the vet, "We need to think this over." We carried our hound out of the clinic and went home.

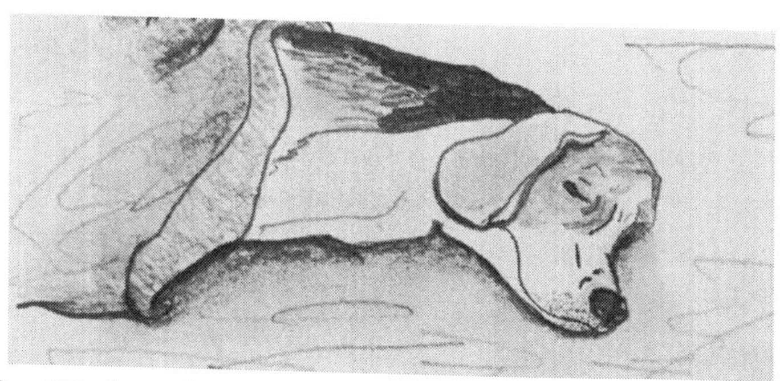

On Wednesday, after we got home, we continued to search the Internet. We had a house meeting that afternoon to let our son, Jay, know what was going on. Jay, ten years old at the time, and Hushie had grown up together and were quite close. He was confident that Hushie would recover. He told us that we could not even consider putting Hushie down.

We called a couple of other vets. We prayed a lot. The one distinct answer was to find experts in animal science. Maybe they could get to the bottom of this mysterious paralysis. That was the least we could do.

We remembered that just a couple of days before, Hushie had briefly gazed at Denise and gave her a small wag of his tail. Even though it was brief, it gave us a glimmer of hope and something to latch onto. Be it ever so small, Hushie had communicated with us in that moment. That was enough to keep us motivated.

We knew Hushie was a friendly and feisty dog, with a boatload of personality. He hadn't given up, no matter what it looked like, so we couldn't give up, either.

We decided to take Hushie to the University of Missouri School of Veterinary Medicine in Columbia. This gave us some confidence since this was one of the premier universities for animal care in the United States. Since it was three hours away and Hushie had continued to show no improvement, we knew we had to move fast. It had now been several days since Hush had fallen into this stupor. I decided to take a couple of days off work to make the trip.

We were running out of time. There was no change. This was our last-ditch effort.

It was just Hushie and me in the car. He remained still and would not eat. I pulled the car over a few times and tried to feed him water by forming my hand into a cup, but he ignored that.

Once I made it to Columbia, I carried him into the vet hospital and described his symptoms. They wanted to test and monitor him for a week. Of course, I had to ask about costs since we didn't have any pet insurance. The estimate was about $1,000. Ouch!

Though unprepared for this hit to our meager savings, I agreed without hesitation.

Time crept along for several days. Because there were no major updates, we started to think that Hushie was a goner.

Towards the end of the week, we got word that Hushie had wagged his tail and that he had taken handheld food. And he'd been taken off the IV, too. We were surprised and thrilled to hear he could come home soon!

It had been seven days since I dropped him off. I couldn't get back up to Mizzou country fast enough. After long days and nights apart, I wondered: Would Hushie recognize me? How would he respond?

As I cracked the door to his caged area, we locked eyes, he wagged his tail, and I let out a belly laugh. What a wonderful moment — one I will never forget.

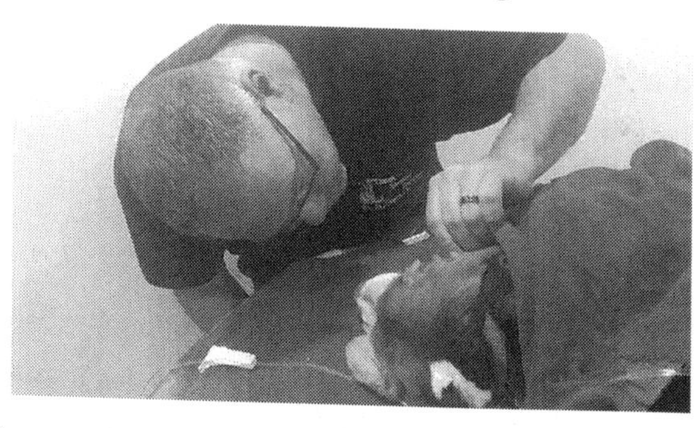

Hushie received multiple medications at the hospital. I was a bit concerned about his travel capability back home, since he still seemed a bit off. There was no certain diagnosis or prognosis from the team of vets. But I knew getting him back home would enhance his healing.

When we drove back over the Missouri River, the sun shone through the rafters on the bridge. It was late in the day and it had an effect of light, dark, light, dark that flashed overhead. It clearly disturbed Hush. He shuddered and howled at the strobe-light effect. It was much like how a soldier tormented by shell-shock would react upon hearing fireworks go off. Seeing this, I knew that Hushie was still not 100%, but obviously he was much improved.

I took solace in the fact that we were both together and heading back to a safe and familiar place.

Hushie walked through the front door on his return. He was warmly greeted by all, but we kept it low-key. He slowly made the rounds of his domain. He would slightly wag his tail here and there. He would stop and offer an occasional assortment of barks if something pleased him. Maybe the best sign that good days were coming is that he knew right where his dog dish was. When he saw it was empty, he gave his patented "fill 'er up" bark.

He seemed happy to be home. After a couple of weeks back in his familiar confines, Hushie seemed to be back to normal. We were all so grateful and we lavished an extra portion of love and attention on him every day. Jay made a bed on the floor at night and cuddled up next to his pal. It was a time of healing for all.

To this day, none of the vets or the staff at the UM Vet Center know what caused his paralysis. Was it a snake-bite? A mole? Did he hit his head while running back and forth next to our fence? (He often did that, provoking and being provoked by George, our neighbor's bulldog.) Was it poison? We don't know, but what matters most is that he came through.

Though that event happened years ago, it taught me a great lesson. What if we had given up on Hushie?

If so, we would have missed out on a lot of life. We would have missed fun experiences and lots of valuable lessons. Our lovable critter exhibited a "never say die" attitude that sticks with me to this day.

Never Give Up

I learned some valuable lessons from Hushie's amazing rebirth. The obvious thing that stands out is to never give up. Never. This is not only on those close to you, but especially on yourself. If you believe in someone or something in your core being, go after it. You need to ride that event or idea through to completion. There will be setbacks, but press forward.

Just like Hushie never gave up, there are many familiar examples of this kind of spirit that we can look to for insight and inspiration. I like to look at the world of sports since it is so prevalent and accessible to us in our society. There are many stories of teams or individuals that pressed though hardship to achieve their dreams.

Here is one that will give you a better idea what I'm talking about. Like Hushie, the Boston Red Sox of 2004 were down and out, it appeared there was little chance for recovery, but then day by day, the big resurgence unfolded.

The Red Sox in the championship series that year achieved one of the most unlikely and remarkable comebacks in sports history. Like Hushie it took place in just over a week that felt like eternity while in the battle. They hadn't won a World Series championship in over eighty years. The "curse" of trading Babe Ruth to the archrival New York Yankees haunted great Red Sox teams for decades. After all, the Yanks went on to win twenty-seven championships after that. In the meantime, Boston players including greats like Ted Williams and Carl Yastrzemski came close, but never achieved the ultimate prize.

Finally, in 2004, the Red Sox got another chance. Of course they were facing none other than their archrival and recent champions, the Yankees. It was a best-of-seven game championship series. There were high hopes again.

A week later, the Red Sox were down three games to none. If they lost one more game, they would be out of the playoffs, and their World Series dreams would end. By the same token all they had to do now was win four straight games against the defending world champions.

The Red Sox were trailing in Game 4 when they began the 9th and final regular inning. They were down to their last chance, or the series was over. Once again, naysayers were already sealing their coffin.

To start the inning, Kevin Millar drew a walk by standout Yankees closer Mariano Rivera. Dave Roberts then came into the game to pinch-run for Millar, and stole second base. Bill Mueller singled, which allowed Roberts to score the tying run. They forced the game into extra innings.

After a few more innings, Boston slugger David Ortiz hit a walk-off home run to win in the 12th inning.

The Red Sox were still alive to play one more game!

Game five was a nail-biter, but Ortiz's single in the 14th inning of Game 5 scored the winning run for Boston. (To add to the drama, Game 5 was the longest post-season game in baseball history.) The Red Sox were now down 3 games to 2.

Curt Schilling started Game 6 for the Red Sox. He had a damaged ankle tendon, but he wanted the ball. He had spent years honing his abilities aiming to get to the mountaintop of the baseball world. He pitched for seven magical innings, allowing just one run. When he left the game, he walked off the mound with his sock covering his injured ankle soaked in blood. He seemed as if he was going to will his team, the Red Sox, to never give up, to never give in, as he exhibited a "never say never" attitude to the extreme. This motivated the team to dig deeper and give it their all.

Perhaps they could turn the tables on the curse.

The Red Sox won Game 6, and became the first baseball team in history to ever force a Game 7 after having been down 3 games to none.

Game 7, unlike the last three games, was not even close. Boston easily beat New York, 10–3, which catapulted the Red Sox to the World Series. For the first time in years, despite all odds, they had another chance at the title.

They carried that "Never Give Up" attitude and momentum into the World Series, defeating the heavily favored St. Louis Cardinals in four straight games, and brought back a trophy to their long suffering fans.

Attitude is everything. Never give up. They didn't. Nor did little Hushie.

But there are still more examples to learn from, this time coming from American history.

President Abraham Lincoln overcame repeated setbacks to become one of the greatest statesmen in the history of the country. His life and character embodied an unquenchable spirit.

Abraham Lincoln

President
of the
United States
of
America

In 1831 his first attempts at business failed.
In 1832 he lost the election for the state legislature.
In 1833 another business venture was unsuccessful.
In 1835 his future wife passed away, practically destroying him. He also lost two children during his lifetime haunting him through his adult life.
In 1843 his election for congress was defeated.
In 1848 he again failed to win a seat in Congress.

In 1855 he failed to win a Senate election.
In 1856 he ran for vice-president and lost.
In 1859 he lost in a state senate election.
In 1860 after many attempts, his perseverance paid off and he became the 16th President of the US.

Step Back and Assess

I learned another lesson from Hushie's extraordinary recovery. That is to look beyond the surface. I need to resist the urge to be hasty. I need to stifle the impulse to judge a situation by appearance alone. It almost always leads to incorrect assumptions.

In Hushie's case, we could have accepted the vet's offer to euthanize our dog. After all, to most this would have seemed a hopeless situation and a humane end. But I am thankful that we took time to consider our gut feeling and pursued other options before giving up. If we had not done this, we would have missed a great deal of life and joy with our puppy.

Because we listened to the still small voice inside and not the tyrannical shout of panic we now have many other amazing Hushie stories to share.

Several years ago on a popular TV show, many people witnessed firsthand the impulsive reactions to passing judgement at first glance. Do you remember the story of Susan Boyle? Whose heart has not been warmed by her spirit? Even after a glamorous makeover, she remained a plain individual. But she also had a beautiful voice, and was overlooked for a long, long time because her outward appearance was unremarkable. If Britain's Got Talent hadn't discovered her, she'd still be a complete unknown, and the world would've lost something beautiful without even knowing it.

But think about her journey from an unknown to being beloved by millions for just one moment, will you? Ms. Boyle had to step on the stage in front of a lively crowd and millions of television viewers. There she was, facing heckling, jeers, and an obvious smirk of disdain from judge Simon Cowell, all because her outward appearance was so plain.

Then she started to sing.

The reactions, response, and results on the faces of everyone in attendance dramatically changed. She sounded angelic and hit notes at both ends of the scale with ease. Her appearance led to presumptions and assumptions about her, just as Hushie's early diagnosis did.

The moral of the story: Don't take everything at face value. Give it a bit of space to breathe.

Hushie's experience reminded me of how I learned this in part years before. Let me offer up the following simple story that has stayed with me, because it is full of common sense.

Back the late 1980s, I worked in an insurance office. In the insurance business, there are always customers who seem to be at the short end of a fuse. After all, they hand over money, and what do you — the agent — give back? Usually nothing tangible but a future promise of protection, which rarely gets utilized!

The agency owner, a seasoned broker, taught me a great lesson that I carry on to this day in my work and for life events. Do not jump to a conclusion or give a knee-jerk reaction, but give your response a day to breathe. (Of course, a life-threatening situation is an exception.) Take that perceived "fire," that threat, that urgent matter that you must react to, and let it – and you – breathe. Take valuable time to sit on it, think it over, and determine a reasoned course of action.

With Hushie, we did not swallow the doctor's advice. We gave it a day to breathe and sought a solution that eventually brought much happiness to our family.

Carry Each Other's Burdens

Hushie, an animal, faced something beyond his ability to bear. What do you do when someone you are close to has encountered a situation beyond their ability to cope with it? How do you know when to step in? How do you decide whether or not this is a real need? (Of course, when a child or a pet has an obvious need, we should immediately respond. They are completely dependent upon us.)

I often go to the scriptures for insight. I have found these verses in the book of Galatians 6:2-5 helpful: "Carry each other's burdens (v.2) .... But each person should carry their own load. (v.5)". These phrases seem to contradict themselves. However the word load in this verse refers to basic responsibility. It means getting a job, showing up to work, paying your bills, cleaning your mess up, etc.

A load, in this context, encapsulates living life, whether it's ever so humble, or whether we are greatly blessed. A burden is something beyond the norm that pushes our capabilities beyond common limits.

As I write this, I am helping a man in a class I teach at church get back on his feet after recently losing his home. He is over sixty, in good shape, but is disabled. It is late spring, and he is living in the bushes out behind the local Walmart. He has all his furnishings stored in a local storage locker. He has a bike, a tarp, and items to keep him warm. This store is open 24/7, so at least in the rain or cold he can sit in the entryway or wander around the store. At this point in our life, Denise and I have no extra room at our INN and our own budget and bills to contend with. We cannot take him in. My load is full.

So what can we do to help him? We have given of our time, given him encouragement, food, and some money for necessities. We have also given him some ideas regarding governmental and church resources that can get him over the hump.

But in the end, he chose to stay outside rather than go to a shelter. A year later I took a class at church about co-dependency and how we can help people to a fault where we enable them. The result is that people often stay stuck and lose their desire to move on. The point here though is that this man truly was up against more than he could bear, just as Hushie was. In his case he stayed stuck, whereas with Hushie the intervention was well-received.

I see this story as a perfect illustration of when to help and to what extent. I am, by the grace of God, carrying my own load and helping a man with a burden beyond his resources and capability. We all need to care a bit more, we need to have compassion for others, we need to look for the opportunity to build others up, then we have to let them respond. In the meantime, we should continue to attend to our own responsibilities and our own family as well. In this way, we will be able to truly help others.

Fortunately, everyone has the right to make their own choices. Even if we do not agree with another's choice, we still need to be patient, help as we can, and then let it go. Even at the vet hospital we had to let go, and fortunately, Hushie came through.

It is remarkable how one event in Hushie's life evoked so much insight. There were three major lessons from one event, which were:

First, Hushie's puzzling dilemma reinforced in me the mindset to never give up. People and pets have more fight in them than we realize.

Next, his near-death experience reminds me to take time to step back and breathe to assess a situation. I don't need to take everything at face value.

Finally, we left him in good hands when we handed him off to the University. It was time to entrust him to others. It was also their burden to bear.

This all can be summed up in the well-known Serenity Prayer, which is generally given as follows:

"God grant me the serenity to accept the things I cannot change, the courage to change the things I can, and the wisdom to know the difference."

I often reflect on the fact that so many great times and stories that follow in these pages would have been missed if Hushie would have been taken early. I — and many others — would have been much poorer, had we not helped Hushie fight for life.

Now that I hope you're interested in my unique pup, let me take you back to the beginning, as to how Hushie came into our lives and changed our world. Some more amazing stories and lessons lie ahead.

Chapter 2

Uniquely You

I've told you a great deal about Hushie's health crisis, but I haven't told you about how Hushie came to be a part of my family. Let me tell you a bit about life with this remarkable animal.

Our neighbor, Tracy Mauk, rescued and fostered stray dogs. With her help, we had tried taking in a rescue pup for a day or two. The owner would always surface, and we felt a strange combination of relief and loss. But we were okay with that, and happy for all concerned. We had not yet experienced that "Eureka moment" when we said, "This is it! This is the match made in heaven."

Besides, I always wanted a Wheaton Terrier. This is a rare find: a large dog, somewhat regal with a uniquely soft and fluffy coat.

It was late September 2004, and Tracy had a new pooch for us to consider. Unbeknownst to me, my wife, Denise, was planning on a big surprise and new addition to our family. Our son, Jay, was now five, and my birthday was days away, so to her it seemed like a perfect time to add a pup to our home.

He arrived amid blaze and shade. It was a sunny, late summer afternoon. The new pup bounded around the yard. Half the time, he got lost in the shadows. He seemed to play hide and seek with the contrasting light and dark. He seemed cognizant of the spell he was putting on us as he engaged us like a professional magician. He was so tiny, his belly dragged across our fresh-cut green grass. He finally plopped down in a heap. He panted, smiled, and wagged his signature tail.

I have never met a beagle that was not charming. This tiny pooch also had a little puppy face to boot. He was about eight weeks old. He was hard to resist. Then he turned around and there it was, a crooked tail; it looked like a lightning bolt. He was so cute but—well, I am embarrassed to admit this—I'd wanted a perfect-looking dog.

Now that I met this lovable puppy, I knew that wasn't going to happen. This new little dog was full of personality, a natural charmer, and he approached me without hesitation. He jumped in my lap and looked at me with big, soulful eyes. He was so soft to the touch. He rolled all over us as I scratched and rubbed him. He enjoyed that so much, he let out friendly yelps that were full of life and joy.

I was in trouble. I had met my match...and possible new companion.

It turns out that this little beagle was half-Basset. I could not see it. Tracy, who rescued him in Ava, Missouri, saw the mother and the rest of the litter and assured us he was half-Basset.

A Basset. Oh no! Strike two.

I'd always imagined a Basset to be a lumbering, slobbering, lazy dog. This dog had a crooked tail and was now a part-Basset to boot.

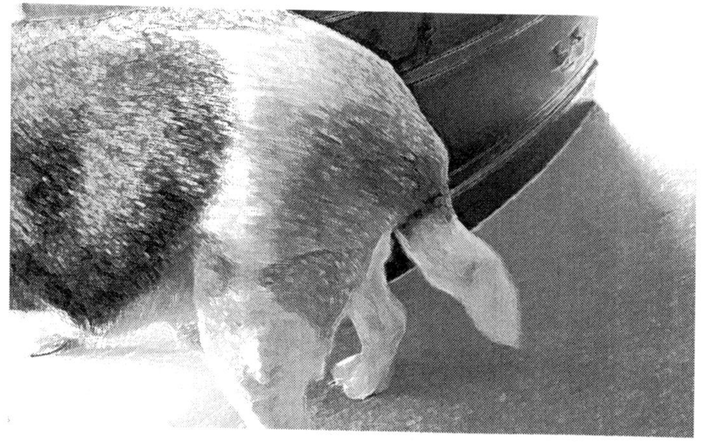

This diminutive dog was also the runt of the litter. But he was also the only one who approached people when called. The rest, all strays, ran. It was obvious they had been abused. Well, at least it was a good sign that he was people-friendly.

I waffled back and forth. Did I want a dog with an obvious blemish? His personality was irresistible, though, so maybe he was a keeper after all.

Have you ever looked into the eyes of a little beagle pup? That was the tipping point. He spent a couple of nights in our house. This little eight-week-old had found a new home, crooked tail and all.

More surprises awaited us, though.

Worms! Like most strays, he had a pretty bad case of them. They had affected his weight, as he was skin and bones. You could feel his ribs right up against his coat when you petted him. The worms caused him to have bouts of diarrhea and vomiting. So, like many parents of newborns, we did our share of cleaning up.

Hushie was full of life and energy. He was always on the move. Always vocal. He had at least ten different sounds and just as many barking tones. What did they all mean? He was an incessant sniffer, too. We should have named him Hoover or Kirby after the vacuum cleaner companies. We also could have named him Bolt for his crooked tail. But we settled on the name Hushie because of the logo of a

beagle pup on the old Hush Puppy shoe boxes. My dad wore those shoes all the time, and I remembered seeing those shoe boxes in the garage with the puppy on the box; that added a bit of nostalgia for me.

He definitely lived to run and play. Unfortunately, sometimes he would run and not come back. He was, after all, a beagle, and with a rabbit in the yard he would definitely *not* come when we called.

Naïve us! He's a beagle!

Now we had a stray, mixed-breed beagle and Basset (our Bagel). He was the runt of the litter and full of worms. Oh yes, all that and with a crooked tail. He was quite imperfect to look at, but just a perfect pet, friend and companion. He found a place in our hearts quickly and our affection for him ran deep.

Thus began a wonderful, long journey of great, warm and endearing moments, for owner and pet alike. Hushie's unique traits, misgivings, and especially his crooked tail taught me some profound lessons.

Embrace Your Perfect Uniqueness

Hushie was completely unfazed by his "shortcomings." That realization led to some productive think time. When I watched Hushie, it reminded me that the less I focus on myself, the better. (The only thing a dog can be self-centered about is, "where is my food?") The more I focused on work, play, rest, and in our human case, others, the better off I'll be.

No one is perfect. The more you get to know someone, the more those imperfections don't matter. They even become unnoticeable, or perhaps endearing. You get to know the real person.

Hushie's "tail condition" made me think about that. Isn't it high time we accepted and embraced our uniqueness?

I have been in the public eye a bit. I have been a speaker and, being in sales, I always meet new people. I've come a long way from my first year in college, where I was so immersed in myself.

Back then, I was so self-conscious, I couldn't even walk into my second semester speech course because I was late for my first class. I felt so intimidated, my body and mind completely seized up. I was afraid of passing out in front of people training to be speakers! I paused, walked on by, and never went to class. How irresponsible. I took an "I" (an incomplete) for the class, which in this case seemed worse than an "F"! It was all about me, and in the end I was the one who suffered.

Then a few years passed. Hard knocks in life ensued, but as a result I had a spiritual awakening. Through that experience I gained enough confidence to go into a room and to speak to a crowd. Even though I'd morphed into a short, fat, old and bald speaker, I could look past that. (I trusted that the crowd would, too!) I reminded myself of the content I brought and wanted them to listen to, rather than worried about the looks of the delivery mechanism. Soon, all the focus on my perceived shortcomings passed, and I never thought about it again.

This brought me to realize that we all have our unique gifts and abilities. Our job is to find them, accept them, nurture them, and focus on *them*, not our perceived shortcomings.

Hushie did that. I saw him in action every day, crooked tail and stout body in tow, following his inborn gift, his nose. It amazed me that he could sniff for hours, tail wagging all the time. I had to believe he liked it. He was fulfilling his calling, doing what he was born to do. It was his joy.

So, how does this apply to you and your life situation? I want you to think about this question: How are you wired? You need to figure that out, and nurture it. Then be persistent. If you are fortunate enough to use your gifts and talents, you will be like Hushie, and enjoy your life.

Accept yourself, and live life to the fullest. Embrace your gifts and your uniqueness.

My gifts and talents, and yours, may not reach and touch thousands or hundreds, but perhaps only a few. Even so, they are still gifts to be cherished. We have to enjoy the space and place in which we are planted. We then just show up and run with it.

We have all heard the phrase, "Do what you love, and you will never work another day in your life!" Such a simple lesson and gift. Hushie was born and lived to chase a scent and he did unabashedly, tail wagging all the while.

Let's take a look at an example of someone you may be very familiar with who exhibited (pun intended) dogged determination to fulfill their gifts and calling in the face of long odds against success. Walt Disney is one of the great men of the 20th Century. But he spent much of his early life buffeted by poison darts from mocking peers. Even his own father hounded him for being a doodler and painter. He was actually fired once by a newspaper because they said he lacked imagination!

But those were not the only misfortunes he encountered. The woman of Walt Disney's dreams severed their relationship, because she thought he would turn into a complete loser. He was always toying with his drawings instead of "getting a real job."

As you can see, there were many moments in Disney's life when he could have given up. He could have called it quits, and fallen to the difficulties of his own life. His dad mocked him, his love left him, and he even lost copyright control over some of his work. At one time he was nearly destitute and living on minimum-wage-level amounts. Despite these setbacks, he managed to build a creative empire.

Today, it is worth tens of billions of dollars. He died knowing that he was one of the artistic icons of the 20th Century. He followed his gifts and interests, showed up to work, and kept at it.

If you can dream it. You can do it.

Walt Disney

Walt Disney and Hushie are great examples to follow. If at all possible, make every effort to do what you love. Find out what you your gift is. Pursue it with all your heart and with purposeful focus. Within that place will be inherent rest.

Trouble is, for most of us life happens, and it makes this idealistic notion tough. Can it be cultivated later in life or midstream? I think so, but not without lifestyle change and sacrifice.

Be Flexible With Your Uniqueness

Let me give you another example, this one drawn from my own life.

I've always loved maps. Our family had maps and atlases all over the house. I learned how to read a map and visualize it very early on. Then, I'd travel in my mind to dream destinations. This was one of my favorite things to do.

I thought it was silly to admit this to my high school counselor when he asked, "What do you like, David?" My silent response, "Ah well, maps," did not seem substantive enough to build a college education on.

Of course, I never 'fessed up.

When I went away to college, I did not know what I wanted to do for a living. I remember standing in the hallway of the Geography Department at the University of Cincinnati. I wanted to talk to the Dean about pursuing geography as a way of life. Forty years later, I can still picture the softly lit hallway and the dark wooden shelving along the walls. I still see the tall ceilings and antique maps chronicling history.

As I stood there, fear and practicality took over. I never pursued that discussion. So, onward I went into the world of business.

Fortunately, we are all wired with multiple aptitudes and abilities. I was able to make use of other interests and talents. But did I feel passion for it deep in my core? Not so much.

I wonder how things would have turned out if I pursued my love of geography and maps. Fortunately, it became a hobby and lifelong pursuit and outlet—in other words, it became an avocation.

Over time, I came to find fulfillment and joy in endeavors related to people. I loved being a catalyst for ideas and solutions to meet business needs. I fulfilled these desires in the world of advertising and technology. One position afforded me a creative outlet, while the other the chance to think and use my mind. So if you can't love everything you do or do what you are good at, embrace and nurture what you can.

And obviously, I also loved being around dogs. It seems from childhood through much of my adult life there was a dog in my life. None had the big personality like Hushie, though.

Everyone is a genius.
But if you judge
a fish by it's ability
to climb a tree,
it will live its
whole life believing
that it is stupid.
—A. Einstein

Hushie lived life full on with his unique characteristics including his great sense of smell and that signature crooked tail. He did not care what anyone else thought. He pulled animals and people into his life and world. He fulfilled his calling, as simple as it was and he and everyone around him were better off for it. We have the same privilege to utilize our God given talents. Our challenge is that it may not come quite as naturally, but the blessing is that once identified we can train and fine tune it and perhaps take it higher.

How can a human discover his own uniqueness? I have found it helps to step out and explore. Find something that gets a hold of you and you will find joy in it. It helps to also be open and honest with those who know you. Sometimes they can identify things we can't. I have taken a lot of tests, surveys, and classes through the years to discern my aptitudes. It has been helpful and insightful to discover nuances about myself and my uniqueness.

In the appendix are a few tools I have used to bring enlightenment to this area of my life. When you get a handle on your identity, gifts, and passion, you just have to follow that.

Follow your heart. The more you nurture that, the more it will come to you as natural, peaceful, and divine.

Of course, a simple starting place is to watch your puppy interact with his world for a day!

Let that beloved pet be an inspiration for you to stir up what lies within you. Then you can give back to the world around you. Just like my friend Hushie. He did so in such unpretentious ways.

Let's take a look at how he did things: simple, yet grand.

Chapter 3

Simplify

About eight years before Hushie came into our lives, Denise and I met through friends we went to church with in New York City. We eventually started dating regularly. She lived on 80th Street on the Upper West Side of Manhattan.

One of our favorite places to go hang out was just a few short blocks away at the dog run in Central Park. (I know that must seem crazy, considering all the wonderful venues in the City!) We both just loved to watch the dogs play and interact there. It became our oasis. We both grew up with dogs and it helped us keep centered and in touch with our roots. Like Hushie in the prior chapter, each dog had unique mannerisms, and it was so interesting to see how they all interacted. It also provided a place of retreat in the busy metropolis that we lived and worked in.

After going out for about six months, we got married and moved upstate to Piermont, NY, about thirty miles away. Three years later in 1999, our son Jay was born. I still commuted into the Big Apple for work every day. Up at 4:30 AM, out the door at 5:15 AM, fists clenched on the steering wheel in my Nascar lineup on the Palisades Parkway in order to beat the 6:30 rush at the GW Bridge. It was a beautiful drive and we loved the City and all the energy, diversity, and opportunity. But we definitely did not love the two-hour commute back home at the end of the day.

We had talked about a simpler, slower life back near our families and figured if we made the move, it would be easier to do it before Jay started school. So in the fall of 2003, we moved back to the Midwest to be near Denise's family in Missouri.

Perhaps we could slow down just a little bit now.

We were also so excited that the time was finally ripe to be able to bring our own unique doggie into the family.

We settled in the Queen City of the Ozarks, Springfield, Missouri. Hushie was with us at that home for one year. He had a big backyard to play in, and we rigged up a 100-foot cable that he could run on. One end was anchored to our back deck and the far end to a jungle gym I built for Jay. We attached a long leash to it and Hushie wore out a path running back and forth on that line.

We had to let him have his freedom from that back and forth run sometimes. With no fences, it made for lots of chases around the neighborhood. This usually culminated at the massive brush pile a few doors down. Hushie loved to chase his prey there. It housed rabbits and hiding places. We even saw a red fox emerge once. We cajoled and corralled Hushie countless times out of that maze of weeds and fallen trees. It was the perfect place for a hound dog to explore.

However, we had to move in order to be closer to Denise's work. So we prepared to relocate to the nearby town of Ozark, which is a small, self -contained community with a historic square and river park.

We loved the area. It had a great school system. Our son, Jay, was going into the second grade. He would have lots of friends to play with in this new, sprawling neighborhood. And it was close to nature. It had rugged hills, beautiful rivers, and many lakes. Jay, like his Dad, loved to get out and explore the beautiful terrain. It seemed like the perfect place for our family.

There would be no colossal brush pile behind this house, though. We wanted to find a house with a fence to keep our pup corralled. We wanted a more lived-in vibe, lots of trees and shrubs on this new plot of land. After a search, we found a home with a lovely manicured backyard. It had trees, bushes, a small pond, a shed, and lots of places to explore for a furry canine. But it had no fence.

A fence was a must. We had to have this little place with the lovely yard for all to enjoy, but a fence would be our first major expense—no, let's rephrase that. The fence became the first investment in our four-legged member of the family.

Twenty-five hundred dollars later, we had a nice privacy fence and about 1/3 of an acre for our hound to wander around in. Finally, we could enjoy playing with him and let him run to his heart's content. This would be his playground, his kingdom, his turf.

One of his many talents and passions that emerged from this venue was playing fetch. Hushie had become a relentless fetcher. I would sit on the back deck and Hushie would bring his ball to me. He would daily offer his loud and persistent bark, indicating that it was time to play. I would throw the ball all over the yard seeking obscure, different places to try to hide the tennis ball. He would bark and bay and bring the ball back in short order every time. He learned to retrieve the ball and put it right into my hand.

This male bonding would go on for hundreds of throws, and if we allowed, thousands. You should see my throwing arm!

Hushie would get adept at ball manipulation. We would put two balls in front of him on the floor and say, "Hushie, fetch." He would take one in his mouth. At the same time, he would push the other one to me with his feet and nose. He looked like an Olympic soccer player pushing the ball toward his goal. We would cry, "Gooooaaaallll!" He wagged his tail harder as if he knew he just scored the winning shot. It was David Letterman "stupid pet tricks" material!

Hush found three passions in his paradise. The first was obviously playing fetch with the ball. He also loved to sniff every blade of grass for who knows what. And his final passion was chasing that ever-elusive rabbit that lived under our shed.

He had a great work "sniff" ethic. In his younger days, he would often spend eight to ten hours a day sniffing every nook and cranny of the yard. It got to the point that I greeted him when I got home with, "How was your work day, Hush?"

Often, Hushie chased the scent of the rabbit that lived in our yard. There are scores of houses in our neighborhood. Several have sheds, and yet this audacious rabbit picked the one with a beagle/Basset. Sinister!

He and Hushie, I guess, had fun through the years. Hushie would start his day sniffing, bellowing, and baying. These were the sounds of the hunt. Hushie incessantly chased the rabbit and his enticing fragrance.

I used to picture the rabbits huddled together in their warren under the shed, the elders instructing their youngsters how to avoid dogs. This was especially comical and ironic since beagles are bred to chase a cottontail. I'm sure after the training they would kick back and have a good laugh at the futility of this determined canine.

Hushie never caught that rabbit, or any others through the years. But I have to believe that pursuing the pesky rabbits gave Hushie joy, because his tail wagged the whole time. The whole eight to ten hours! I think he sealed each day up as one happy hound.

By the time 2007 rolled around, Jay was in school all day and we both worked, so Hushie was left alone often. We felt it was time for Hushie to have a new companion and teammate to help him chase the rabbit. So after we had been in our Ozark home a year, we got a Golden Retriever puppy from one of Denise's friends. Golden Retrievers have an inborn friendly disposition, and we thought that one might be a good companion for Hushie. And our fenced yard could keep both dogs enclosed safely while being left alone for several hours at a time.

Once we met the rambunctious six-month-old puppy named Lottie, we were taken in by her beauty and sweet demeanor. We brought her home, and she and Hushie took to each other right away. Because of her sweet personality, Hushie never had to exert his dominance. There was no question, though, that he was top dog.

It was surprising that right from the beginning Hushie let Lottie drink out of his bowl at the same time he did. This is no small feat for an alpha male dog. She would get hot spots in the summer, and Hushie would lick them for hours to the point that they healed. They got along well and made for a great team.

But despite their combined stealth, cunning, and persistence, they still could not corner the annoying rabbit!

Hushie had another playmate in those younger days, too. Hushie and Jay, our youngster, the true alpha male of the pack, would often play hide and seek. Jay would pretend to be Tarzan. He would create a loincloth from two tea towels held together by a stretch band. The loincloth replaced his underwear. Jay would take the cushions on the couch and pillows from the bedroom and build a fort.

Hushie wanted to play, too. He would chase Jay, and they would wrestle and have a grand time.

One day, Hushie was chasing Jay as he headed up the stairs. All in fun, Hushie jumped up and pulled the loincloth off Jay from behind. Denise saw it and videotaped it. She was sure that it should be submitted to the America's Funniest Videos TV show. To save Jay embarrassment, we held back, but we all had a great laugh.

Playful events like this endeared Hushie to us. He had become a part of the family. It was touching to see Jay and Hushie after a time of exuberant play, limbs entangled as they lay together on the floor. They ended up piled in a heap entering into that wonderful place we call rest.

Of course, rest is a definite natural by-product of hard work and hard play. Dogs eat, sleep, and play. Like kids, play is their work.

It seems the biggest part of their day, though, is sleep (rest). A simple life: play, work and rest.

I am not sure if our move from New York to Missouri slowed us down much. It wasn't until I started interacting with our dogs that I began to realize they had a lot to offer me with simplifying my life. I just had to slow down enough to listen before I could learn from them.

Why? Well, learning takes place when we not only gain knowledge, but when we put that knowledge into practice. Let's check on my progress for this one.

Keep It Simple

Play. Work. Rest. Hushie had his priorities down. How do you prioritize these?

As a young person, play is the priority. As a teen, perhaps rest is, although your parents may call it lazy. Through the majority of your life, work consumes the most time. It is often the focus of our life.

When we greet one another, we don't ask "What is your hobby?" or "What do you like to do?" We ask, "What do you do for a living?" Work rules an adult's life.

There are seasons in life, or places in the world, where these three simple events may be hard to achieve. Nonetheless I turn back to one of God's creations, the hound, as an example for us. Although developed and bred by mortals, hounds can bring enlightenment to the human soul.

This next lesson has become clear to me the older I have gotten. It is the most challenging for many. I had no problem in my youth and teen years fulfilling my play and rest requirements! Aside from standard chores, my parents were gracious, lenient, and not demanding. They let us kids be kids. (I was glad, because it was a short window.) In my teens and early twenties, I found that sports and nature gave me great joy. I could join in, observe, and enjoy that environment.

Hushie had his terrain to wander, and I had mine, too. One of my favorite things to do was to go canoeing. Nothing brought me closer to nature, God, and perhaps my true fulfilled self than a day on the river. In my younger days I would often go down to the Little Miami River, in Ohio, and enjoy that scene. There were eddies, riffles, even a couple of Class One rapids. I especially enjoyed the long, still stretches. I would lay back and float and enjoy the sun streaming through the tree cover.

I always enjoyed the water (even when I lived in Ohio), and I wanted to blend this passion with a work environment. In my early twenties I made a repeated effort to get employment at the Ohio Department of Conservation, but to no avail.

Through the ensuing years, something happened. Necessary things called bills, marriage, a child, and of course work demanded my attention. As I look back over the years, I saw that simplicity had slipped away.

And not just in my life, either. I saw it all around me.

Look at our culture, for example. It is in the throes of a paradigm shift, with technology ruling our life. Simplicity has started to disappear. Sure, I love a new gadget as much as the next guy, and I consider myself an early adopter. But there must be time to be away from technology, and that seems to get harder and harder to attain the older I get. Especially from the mid to late 1990s, I have sensed the passing of an uncomplicated life.

Maybe it's that I am morphing into an older, responsible adult, but I hear the same sentiment every week in casual conversations. "My life is too busy," folks say. I see it in their eyes and hear it in their urgent tones. How paradoxical, since technology is supposed to make our lives more efficient.

I don't think anyone realizes the extreme pace of change that has accompanied technology. Have you been bombarded with a plethora of devices to help enjoy life, perhaps simplify it? Do all of these fancy applications solve a deep need to simplify and get back to the big three of play, work, and rest?

So far, it has been tenuous for me. I see it, and perhaps have touched and tasted it. I have had enough of a sampling of the simplified life to know I want and need more. I long to sit under a tree with a fishing pole dangling in the water, cell phone turned off and happily catching nothing!

Where did the harmonious balance of these three key elements in life go? That of play, work, and rest. How can we get our equilibrium back?

Ah, yes, we must turn again to our beloved companions. Perhaps in observing them, we'll find our own answers.

One day, I rushed home from work on a Friday. I was trying to beat a rainy weekend to get the grass cut. I rushed my mower through the backyard. The wonderful late afternoon sun shone through the trees, creating delightful pockets of shade I loved. It was over 90 degrees. I was sweaty, cranky, rushed, and taking it out on the grass blades.

I kid you not, I looked over at the other side of the yard, where Hushie and Lottie were laying together in the shade. There just seemed to be something wrong with this scene. Then I had a lightning bolt revelation. It looked like they had smirks on their faces! As if they were communicating with each other, something to the effect of, "When will this human learn?"

Learn what?

It hit me that something needed to change. The dogs needed to be out here cutting the grass, while I watched them in my lounge chair while sipping an iced tea!

But we know that is not possible.

How did this little runt of the litter and his sidekick get me to ponder my priorities?

In our fast-paced, ever-changing world, keeping it simple is of supreme importance. Life is chaotic and complex. More information is coming at our young people than existed in all of recorded history. We need order to keep this data overload manageable. Let's see what that might look like.

Focus

I often observed Hushie at work as he sniffed and bayed. I was awestruck at his focus. One day, in another revelation, I realized where the term dogged determination came from. To this day, eleven years later, he has yet to catch that elusive rabbit.

But do you think he is giving up? Not a chance. It is in his wiring. He is a worker, even though it looks unproductive.

This next quote may seem strange, but it does apply to Hushie if you think about it long enough. Hushie spent many a day head-down and with one determined purpose in mind: to catch that rabbit.

Thomas Edison, the inventor of the light bulb and renowned for his hard work, said,

"Opportunity is missed by most people, because it is dressed in overalls and looks like work."

Hard work. Now that is a bright idea!

Balance

I have no doubt that Hushie worked hard, but I believe he mastered the work-life balance challenge. He did not let his work take over his life.

But how are the rest of us supposed to do this?

Can we learn from Hushie's example? And if so, how?

Because we need to do just that. In the ever-changing maze of our fast-paced 21st Century world, we tend to get wrapped up in everything going on all around us and forget "the big three." Maybe you are fortunate and have found your gifts, of course you work hard, and...do you ever remember to "unplug" or tune out?

Most of us in this day and age forget to rest, and perhaps forget to take time to play as well.

I worked in the fast-paced world of technology. I struggled with the work-life balance. The volume and swiftness of information had a tsunami-like affect. What I loved about the work was that it was mentally stimulating. What I hated about the work was that it was mentally stimulating!

It was too mentally energizing and draining! It was all too much, too fast with something new and urgent every week, if not daily. So the challenge of the peaceful, ordered life often got compromised. I learned that it takes concentrated thought and effort to make sure I build rest into my life. That scene in the backyard mowing in a rushed huff was just what I needed.

Dogs show us the way to live a full and simple life. None of us will be on top of our game if we don't pause, step back, and regroup.

How would you feel if your surgeon came in exhausted before your surgery? How would you feel if your pilots announced over the loudspeaker how stressed and tired they were before they started to fly the airplane you're on?

You want to enjoy life and live a few more years, go mimic a hound.

Work hard. Play hard. Combine these two if possible. Finally, rest well.

Keep it simple. Sometimes, you may have to be proactive and plan for it. These are major lessons that I will continue to have to work on and true up from time to time. But the point is they are taken and accepted...thanks to Hush and Lottie!

Chapter 4

Survive or Thrive?

So far, these stamps were on Hushie's life: abandoned; stray; crooked tail; paralysis; left for dead. But instinctively and naturally, Hushie overcame all obstacles.

But that, unfortunately, was about to be challenged again.

Sometime in 2013, we noticed that Hushie was getting sluggish. We didn't think a lot about it at first since he was getting a bit older. He was overweight. His belly hung a little bit lower than before and he had a wide physique. We attributed all that to his Basset heritage. Then he started to lose control of his bladder, usually in the wee hours of the morning. Again, we thought this was age, but we were wrong.

One night he had a severe seizure that shook his whole body. We noticed when he got up that he seemed to have trouble getting and keeping himself oriented. He seemed to move about the house a bit more gingerly. Was it old age or something else?

Jay identified it first, but we finally all realized that Hushie was going blind. After eight years of navigating our house and yard, he had compensated for his loss of eyesight by relying on his memory and keen sense of smell. He had fooled us for a long time, navigating around his "hood."

The vet confirmed that Hushie was losing his sight and the cause was diabetes. He was prescribed two shots of insulin per day. This was in 2013, and he was only nine years old.

One Saturday afternoon in the summer of 2014, I watched as Hushie bumped into a wall while making his way to the back door. He got to the door, tail wagging so hard it shook his whole body (and, as a result, the genesis for this book). Despite losing one of his key senses, eyesight, his attitude had not been affected.

Then it hit me, square and clear. My blind dog still wagged his tail!

What a revelation. Despite a major setback and limitation in his senses, Hushie still carried on in life with a great, tail-wagging attitude.

It was interesting to watch Hushie's progression into visual darkness. You could see the cloudy, bluish cataracts slowly take over his eyes. He intuitively counted the steps walking around our house. I imagined that the different textures of tile and carpet give him clues. He may have thought, Okay, turn here for my water dish. Or, Okay, here is the plastic that covers our carpet near the back door.

Our backyard was beautiful, one of my favorite places to just chill out. It was a peaceful and serene setting for man and beast alike. Hushie and I enjoyed it as a safe haven where we had many wonderful bonding moments.

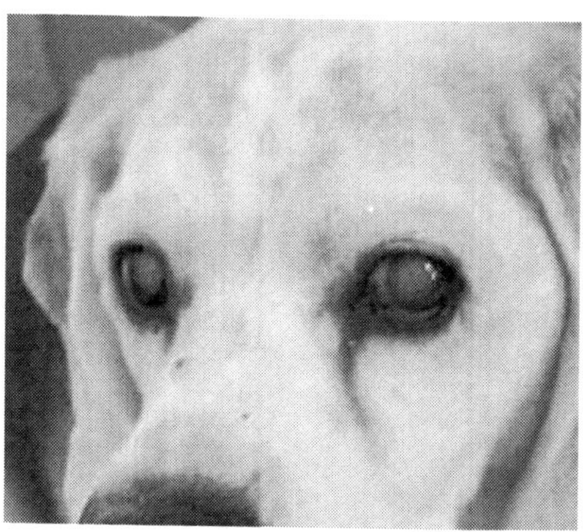

For a blind dog, though, it had some hurdles to overcome. First, we realized that the steps off the deck could cause Hushie to stumble. There were sassafras trees clumped in groups around the yard that might cause him trouble, too -- they could have definitely stopped Hushie in his tracks. Since we needed to give Hushie some help, but didn't want him to feel less than he was, we decided to plant bushes around the perimeter of the fence. Those served as barriers or reminders.

We also had a shed, bordered by rose bushes, honeysuckle, a lilac bush, peonies, and all kinds of ground cover. We had raised garden beds and a good-sized compost heap behind the shed. Through the years, we had to put big boulders around the shed. Why? Because Hushie, especially, and Lottie would work like a mini-wolf pack trying to catch that crazy rabbit hidden underneath. They would scratch and claw the earth and move stones half their size to try to reach their prize.

Through the years, Hushie learned this landscape like the back of his hand. Though nearly blind, he still traversed it like he owned it. We had full confidence he could still be left alone safely all day to enjoy the great outdoors.

Adjacent to the shed was a big center island with more trees, along with various plants and bushes, including hydrangeas and daffodils that Hush would lie in. Near the back deck and house was a long privacy hedge, still one of his favorite places to cool off. Then topping off this blind man's obstacle course was our small, gated fish pond and our fire pit surrounded by outdoor furniture.

Can you visualize this scene and the challenges facing a creature that has lost his sight? You'd think Hushie would be daunted, wouldn't you? But despite all these impediments, he carried on with sniffing the ground and chasing the rabbit (who always vanished).. With energy to spare, he still asked to play fetch, using his great sense of smell to find the ball anywhere in his jungle paradise -- tail wagging non-stop.

We always wore out before he did, and said, "No more, Hushie!" We moved our hands back and forth across our neck as if he could still see this gesture to indicate that we were done. On that command, he promptly stopped and dropped to the ground, sprawled his back legs out and rest-ed, chewing on his prize catch. His tail was still wagging cheerfully, another great day in the books, despite a "minor" inconvenience of loss of sight.

Strength in Weakness

What do we do when life happens and throws us a curveball? You can be smoothly sailing along in life. Perhaps you have found that fulfilling career, or balanced your life to perfection. Then your world collapses all around you. You have been blindsided.

Perhaps man's best friend can teach us something?

Humans and dogs utilize sight differently. For humans, sight is perhaps our most valued sense. For a dog, it is probably second to smell. Nevertheless, it still was a major setback for our Hushie.

Over time Hushie lost the complete use of his sight. He carried on, even though he often bumped into things.

Hushie was moving forward, he was not moping, and he was still happy. Wow! Despite it all, he was still wagging his tail. He was an overcomer, and I found that very inspirational and encouraging.

Sure, human beings have much more complex psyches, but just seeing how another creature dealt with a major setback gave me hope.

Examples abound in our human existence of folks who have overcome adversity, but it still helped me to see Hushie at work, sniffing the yard, and enjoying his life.

Michael Jordan was perhaps the greatest athlete and champion of his generation. He was extremely gifted and he worked extremely hard. But the beginning of his basketball career started very differently. He was actually cut from his high school basketball team.

What a setback.

He took it to heart and unleashed a single-minded focus to improve, which served as the core of his motivation and drive. He did not allow a temporary roadblock diminish the purpose he was created for. He thrilled and inspired many by the giving of his great talent and by his great heart, fortitude and achievements.

Maybe it seems odd to compare Hushie to Michael Jordan, but I see the parallels. (Don't you?). A major set back, but both pressed on. Hushie was a blind dog who still wagged his tail. He carried on and became a blessing to me and my family, and in turn to others.

But I see other parallels to well-known individuals, too. For example, Helen Keller had major obstacles to overcome. She was deaf and blind. She became a world-renowned author and humanitarian who did amazing things with her life. She was born normal, but contracted a disease at nineteen months of age that radically changed the course of her life. Over time and with great effort, she learned to read and write. She eventually graduated from college. She became a spokesperson for civil rights, particularly women's suffrage. She accepted her challenges and then reached out to the world to give of her heart and soul.

She said the following in her article for American Foundation for the Blind, "Dreams That Come True":

"I seldom think about my limitations, and they never make me sad. Perhaps there is just a touch of yearning at times, but it is vague, like a breeze among flowers.

But there are still more well-known individuals' lives I'd like you to consider.

Jim Abbott was a professional baseball pitcher for the New York Yankees, and he once pitched a no-hitter. What makes it extraordinary is that Jim did all this despite being born with only one hand.

The following quotes are from Jim's book *Imperfect: An Improbable Life*: *"Find something you love, and go after it, with all your heart."* (Sound familiar?)

Later, he said, *"I worked very hard. I felt I could play the game. The only thing that could stop me was myself."*

Jim also mentioned, *"The Bible says be grateful in every situation. I am grateful for mine."*

But I have yet another example for you.

What happens when you are a healthy and vibrant young person such as Joni Eareckson Tada and life deals a devastating blow? Joni has been a quadriplegic since a diving accident in 1967. She is now known internationally as a mouth artist, bestselling author, and inspiration for millions. She has learned how to look beyond the devastating results of her injury and open herself to God and a whole new realm of possibilities. She humbly admits that it is the grace of God that has transformed her.

Of course it has not been easy, as nothing worthwhile ever is. Many people would not have been able to overcome what Joni has, much less be able to find new talents in the process.

"We will stand amazed to see the top side of the tapestry and how God beautifully embroidered each circumstance into a pattern for our good and His glory." -- Joni Eareckson, *Heaven: Your Real Home*

There is a common denominator I see in all these examples. The mental attitude is positive. The energy is outward. The eternal perspective is upward. Consider these as essential elements to living in victory. Each person refused to be trapped by reflecting back on what could have been or should be. They learned that if you keep looking inward at yourself without looking up or reaching out, you will stay stuck.

Of course, sometimes you have to struggle for a long time to understand your changed circumstances. That struggle shouldn't be overlooked, as it is of great value. Think of you and your struggle like coal that has been compressed for thousands of years in order to become a precious diamond. That is what you are!

Remember, never give up, keep your faith, and have the heart to reach out to others along the way.

It's very challenging to live up to the attitude of these examples, but isn't it inspiring as well?

We Have a Choice

Honestly, one of my ongoing struggles is with negativity. I can jump to an apocalypse mentality if I don't manage my mind. But whenever I've looked at my blind dog wagging his tail, I am quietly reminded that I have a choice. My decision has real and impactful consequences. I have a choice to look for the silver lining.

Joni Eareckson, Jim Abbott, Helen Keller and Michael Jordan demonstrated an amazing ability to adapt. Sometimes events and circumstances don't make sense, and are terribly difficult. Perhaps you feel despair or you have no hope. It may seem too simple, but remember what these people have demonstrated.

Look up and reach out. Just give it a try today. Right now, in one of your challenging situations, give it a go.

I like this quote from the Apostle Paul of Tarsus:

"Don't worry about anything; instead pray about everything; tell God your needs; and don't forget to thank Him for His answers. If you do this, you will experience God's peace, which is far more wonderful than the human mind can understand. His peace will keep your thoughts and your heart quiet and at rest as you trust in Christ Jesus." Philippians 4:6-7 TLB

We are mere mortals and people in progress, but these are wise words to aspire to.

Chapter 5

Full of Grace

What was it about dogs in God's original design? Why do you think they exist? Is it only to be a friend, or can it also be to teach us about life? Ask the recipient of a service dog's attention what they think. Perhaps they can teach us all just a lesson or two. As much as I love my dog Hushie, I know he's not the only amazing dog out there

Do you know the story about Hachiko? It is a true story of a dog, a golden brown male Akita Inu, a Japanese breed from the mountains of northern Japan. Hachiko was born in 1923 and sold to a well-to-do family in Tokyo while still a puppy. The father of this family, Eisaburo Ueno, was a Tokyo University professor. He was in his fifties when he adopted Hachiko. He loved Hachiko very much and doted on him, as most loving pet owners do. From word-of-mouth tradition, Mr. Ueno took Hachiko for long walks, and treated him as one of the family

Mr. Ueno and Hachiko walked to the train station every workday. After the father went through the train stalls, Hachiko walked back home by himself. Then he would return, every day, to wait outside the stalls to meet Mr. Ueno as he came home. The locals and train station people knew that Mr. Ueno and Hachiko had a special relationship.

One day, Professor Ueno died while he was teaching at the university. Hachiko went to greet him, but he never came. All of the Professor's train mates were aware of the situation. They all wished they could let Hachiko know what happened. They comforted the loyal friend the best they could. At the end of each day as the sun was setting, Hachiko would slowly walk his familiar trail back home. One wonders what was going through his mind day after day.

But that was not the end of Hachiko's story.

You see, for the next nine years, Hachiko continued to walk to the station in the late afternoon. At just the right time, he arrived to meet the train that should have carried his master.

Hachiko's fame grew all over the country, as this kind of love and devotion was unheard of between man and dog. He became the standard bearer for loyalty among a people that highly favored that quality. Over time, millions of people, many of whom passed through the station every day, adored him.

Now, as to how I found out about him? My wife and I visited Japan early in our marriage and stood next to Hachiko's statue. It stands prominently near the train station in the middle of busy, bustling Tokyo. As people scurried about, we would occasionally speak with commuters and listen to their stories. Most spoke about Hachiko in a way that made his story sound bittersweet, yet as everyone spoke they beamed with pride.

This led to some wonderful contemplation on my part. A person would be hard-pressed not to look at their own life and priorities after hearing about Hachiko. This wonderful animal was a constant reminder of love and loyalty, and dedication. His story has not only been endearing, but has encouraged and challenged millions. He is now revered in Japan.

As wonderful as Hachiko was, he's not the only dog who's done something extraordinary.

Have you seen images or heard stories of a dog at the grave-side of a fallen master? (There is something amazing about dogs and the sixth sense they possess.) The former, benevolent master is six feet underground. How is that possible that they know? Isn't this the epitome of loyalty? As well as a demonstration of this mysterious sixth canine sense?

How do such incredible attachments happen? It's a great mystery, but it's one I am eager to explore.

Most dogs are inherently cute. They have personalities. They have souls. Given time and attention, they form connections to touch the heart. With our Hushie, it was not only all the adversity he overcame but his bigger-than-life personality that impacted us. His energy and joy drew us in. He, too, was incredibly loyal, which of course was endearing.

The kind of loyalty witnessed in Hachiko is a demonstration of grace. In this sense, grace is receiving better than we deserve. This is a beautiful gift to pet owners in particular. If we allow our pet to love and be loved, we often find they have a great capacity to keep giving. Treated right, dogs will keep on loving their master and tribe members beyond what we might generally give back to them. It is inbred in them, and we end up enjoying the benefits.

We are the recipients of this gift of grace. It reminds me in a small way of God's unparalleled grace extended to us through His Son. Perhaps part of God's design and wisdom here lies in front of us, sitting at our feet, a daily object lesson to open and warm our hearts to greater truth.

I am so grateful for all the many experiences from my own bigger-than-life Hushie. Not the least of which was being greeted daily with a friendly pant, wagging tail, and perky bark.

Along the way, I learned other extraordinary things about Hushie. For example, Hushie was very good at both forgiving and forgetting. Again, I believe these traits are inherent in every dog that has been raised in a friendly environment. I would, also, label these as real-life demonstrations of grace.

Why is this important? Well, if you think about it, owners often have to do things dogs probably don't like very much.

For example, Hushie had to learn not to bite while playing. As a puppy, it was fun and harmless. He was showing his fondness by gnawing away at a finger or toe. But in time, his behavior had to be confronted and changed, else he could've inflicted pain or injury on us or houseguests. Hence, it is the responsibility of the owner to train and domesticate the pet. And that's a process most pets—Hushie included—don't like. He had no concept of the hurt he could inflict on an unassuming houseguest. So there had to be a pause in playtime in order to stop all his high-spirited momentum so he'd not unintentionally hurt someone.

When Hushie was younger, as with most dogs, he had to be housebroken. We were vigilant, and always did our best to catch him before he was about to "do his business" in the house. Catching him quickly helped him understand that he needed to go outside to eliminate. There were many teachable moments like this that eventually led to acceptable behavior.

Sometimes, though, he wouldn't make it in time. We would use our strong, correcting voice. He would hide his tail before slinking off in shame. Fortunately, he soon returned to normal. And better yet, in time he changed his behavior!

All along the way there were never any ancillary issues or emotions in tow. He was free and clear emotionally. He was able to leave the confrontation in the past. He forgot about it.

What a great lesson!

Now, it has become a habit. He doesn't show any guilt, he doesn't harbor a grudge, and he continues to love me and my family despite the fact we had to discipline him many times before he got the idea (smart dog though Hushie always was, he could be incredibly stubborn, too).

In other words, forgiving and forgetting can be both a developed habit and a grace-given character trait.

If you think about it, these are wonderful, simple lessons from man's best friend, if we would just slow down and take a bit of time to consider them.

Extend Grace To Others

All these examples from Hachiko and Hushie made me wonder. How can I be more loyal? How can I be more loving? An obvious answer is to invest in others more. There has to be an object to give and receive those demonstrations of grace. Isn't that what these dogs did with their masters and families?

Imagine if your spouse came home every day and was able to think about you and your relationship rather than how bad his or her day was. Wouldn't that be great?

Think about it. If they weren't stewing or troubled about their day, even if there were substantial problems, and they focused on you and your marriage, wouldn't that be something we all should aspire to?

Yes, there are many problems in this life we must deal with. But if for just thirty seconds your spouse would give you a spontaneous, welcoming greeting, wouldn't that be better than what most of us get?

Think about a loyal, loving dog greeting his or her master at the door after a long, hard day at work. Usually, a dog wags its tail, bounces around, and looks to be in joyous rapture that you're home. This shows that you were missed and that you are appreciated for being who you are – and isn't that what we want?

Yes, people don't wag tails, and people don't tend to bounce around, as that's much more natural for a dog than for a human being. But that loyalty and love, and the feeling of welcome support, is something that can transform us and others.

No wonder we love dogs so much.

Keep in mind, some people are already working on this idea. One of my friends, Ed Hultgren, has been married for thirty years. He once told me that all he ever asked for from his bride was a smile when he came through the door. Simple! She did it and does it (and I am sure she, Andrea, takes a day off now and then, too!)

What a great, simple formula. Let's greet each other like a dog does their master! Can you imagine the impact?

Forgive

Another lesson is a bit more divine. Going back to the ability to forgive and forget, scientists say a dog has the mind and reasoning of about a two-year-old. If they are exceptional, like our Hushie, a four-year-old! (I just had to throw that in.) That is, dogs are in a sense too young emotionally to understand a hurt or an offense. The fact is, they do have emotions. They can be happy, sad, defiant, angry, etc.

But both dogs and children have a God-given capability to let water roll off their backs.

Sometimes, that is a great quality to have, as you're about to see.

Recently, an unforeseen, unfortunate, and tragic event challenged my ability to forgive. My youngest brother, Kenny, lost his life in May 2015 due to a violent domestic altercation with his girlfriend. Apparently, he was defenseless, and did not fight. We still don't know all the details, but he may have been sleeping when this happened. This is based upon the police report. It was a horrific scene that left me shocked, sorrowful, confused, and outraged.

Strangely, I also felt pity for the woman, and saddened that she would have to deal with the dreadful aftermath of her actions the rest of her life. I also did my best to both understand and forgive her. I have to believe this has divine roots, as it is beyond my normal response.

But it's also a choice. I have to trust that the emotions will work their way out.

As I write this, since it is so recent, I haven't talked to the woman yet—and I don't intend on doing so, either. But because they spent about a year together. I would like to know her insights about my brother, especially how he was doing his last weeks and days on Earth. But so far, the thought of interacting with her is not appealing.

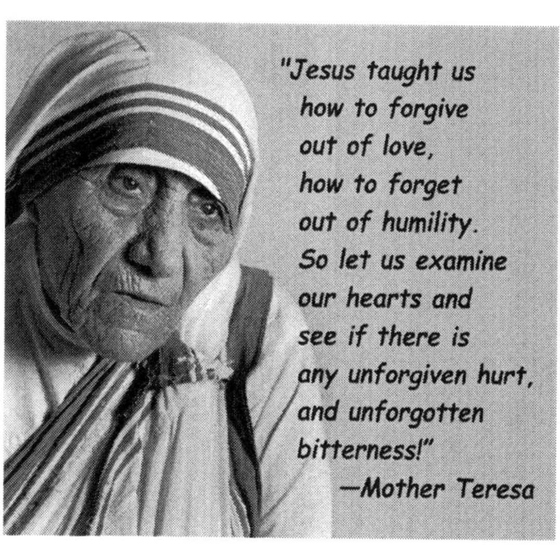

Jesus said to love your enemies. I am not there yet, but I have full confidence if He wants me to be kind and loving to this person I will get there, by faith. In and of myself I cannot do it, but God has the power to deliver a transformation of the heart and mind. All achievable, in due season. We take a step and then the next step. Step by step. Grace meets us as we take the steps and actions.

But how does this relate to dogs, especially my dog Hushie? Maybe it has to do with the whole idea of forgiving and forgetting.

What happens when a dog does something bad? Well, my dogs, after being corrected, tend to act in a very distinctive way. Whether getting into the garbage or eating the cat's food, they respond immediately with a guilty look, heads down, and might even slink off with their tails tucked in. Then, a few minutes later, they exude a behavior that demonstrates, "hey, I heard you, and I learned."

This may sound like an odd thing to observe, but bear with me. In a sense, don't we all get on the hamster wheel of repeated missteps and mistakes? A dog's attitude and response to repeated criticism is so refreshing. They take the correction and meld it with an extraordinary ability to move on. They are not going to stay "guilted out" over it, and refuse to wallow in self-pity.

Sometimes I use my harsh "master's voice" to discipline my pups. A few minutes later, they approach me with a "can I jump in your lap now and lick your face?" look, though, and I indulgently forgive them.

True forgiveness and love never keeps a record of wrongs. That doesn't mean we don't learn, mind you, but you have to remember not to repeat it. Don't ruminate. Get past the rehashing, and refrain from dumping out the gunnysack and bringing up an offense from the past.

Here is a thought, the dogs turned their focus on the master, perhaps we should take note. We can turn our focus on our Master. We can allow that interaction to help us put things in perspective. We can look at things around us that fuel the positive, as they are all around us. Breathe in the fresh air. Feel the warm sunshine as it hits your face. Enjoy the tickling feeling as a blade of grass gets between our toes. Revel in finding a cool spot on a hot summer day, or a warm air vent to sit near on a cold winter night. Or how about appreciating a bowl of food and a cold drink of water? Or one of my favorites: savor a hot cup of coffee in the morning before you have to start the day.

Attitude is everything.

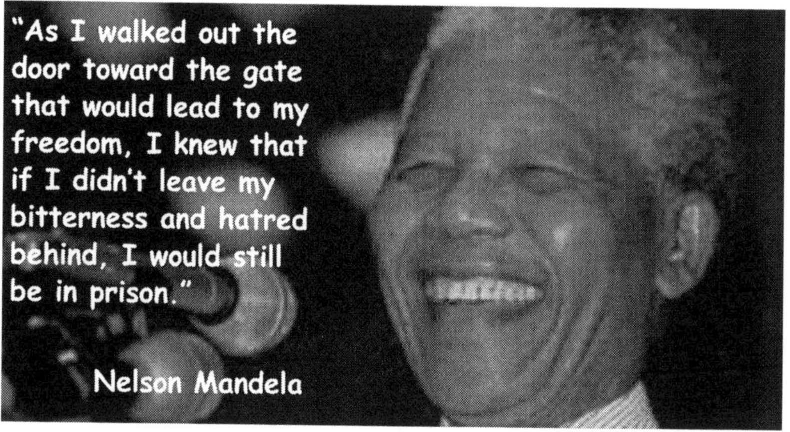

But we have to work at it a bit harder than our canine companions. Still, we need to dwell on whatever is pure and lovely rather than the things that vex and irritate us, or we're missing out on the whole point of life.

Oh, for us to have such a simple brain and heart as my lovely dog, Hushie!

These are great lessons, and we need to appreciate them and seek to inculcate them into our lives.

To sum up: Act quickly. Don't let things get buried or stew. Own it and apologize. Don't keep rehashing it. Learn the lesson. Move on. Last, but not least remember to forgive and especially forgive yourself, that is often the hardest one to forgive. I know I need to get a hold of that one.

Think about this for a moment. Isn't this a good way to live? How divine and humane -- and can we also say, how canine!

Chapter 6

Let's Just Get Along

I am inspired by many other things and people, but oddly enough, they all remind me of Hushie or vice versa. Later in this chapter we will see several dogs put into practice what Rodney King's famous words cried out for, "Can't we all just get along?" As I write this in 2015, our nation is still gripped with racial tension and many inequalities in our society. It is causing fear, anger, uncertainty, and doubt.

In 1991, police stopped Rodney King as he sped through congested Los Angeles. The high-speed chase came to a halt in the middle of a busy intersection. When Mr. King got out of his car, he was beaten without mercy by four officers.

Fortunately, across the intersection, a bystander videotaped the scuffle. (This was one of the first taped recordings by a bystander of an event like this.) The video was taken to a local TV station. In short order, it was broadcast around the world.

Because Mr. King was black, this beating drastically heightened racial tensions. Even worse, more riots broke out in LA after the jury's verdict came back, as it was not favorable toward Mr. King. The results were severe. It culminated in 53 deaths, many injuries, more than 7,000 fires and over $1 billion dollars in damage.

Despite some peaceful protests, the fact was clear that there was great discord in LA and the nation. It was during this time that Rodney King made his famous plea, “Can’t we all just get along?”

Why am I mentioning all this? Because I want to point out that dogs, unlike people, are often more forgiving and understanding when a crisis ensues. First, I need to give you a little background before I explain how these two are connected—Rodney King and Hushie. With Mr. King, there was a dissonance that was enveloping our country; with Hushie, well, he had to forge peace with some newfound antagonists. Let me show you how that unfolded in our home.

Several years after we introduced Lottie to Hushie, we took in another furry creature –this time, one of the feline species. Denise’s grandmother had come to live with us and had a cat in tow. She and Jay christened him Yellow Feathers, named after his gold coat and reflecting pride in her Native American heritage.

Yellow Feathers was not your ordinary house cat. He was a stray, a Garfield lookalike hardened by a life on the streets and shores of the Lake of the Ozarks. Grandma lived next to her brother right on the lakefront. The cat would often get on his property and into the garage and shed. He used to take potshots at Yellow with a BB gun. So especially around men, it took this cat a long time to open up and trust. The corner of one ear was chewed off, due to a battle with a raccoon, dog, or another cat. He was not friendly and quite standoffish.

From her deathbed, Denise's ninety-four-year-old grandmother asked us to look after him. She had an old fashioned name, Beulah Mae, and she had a no-nonsense, old fashioned way about her, too. She was a straight shooting, take-no-guff-from-anyone type of woman.

We figured, "Well, if those two got along, maybe we can figure something out for Yellow and our dogs." But I was worried about Hushie, as he was particularly territorial and did not like change.

Of course, there were incidents where Hushie got clawed by Yellow, and others where Hushie (quite understandably) growled at the cat in return. There was always something to work through. I can imagine Hushie thinking, What path are you going to take, Yellow? Oh, okay, I'll go the other way. Or sometimes, I'm sure Hushie was thinking, Hey, cat, you're getting attention and I'm not. I will come over to this side of my master and remind him I'm here. Sometimes, it was an issue where Denise and I swore Hushie's body language just screamed, Yellow, what are you doing? That's my bed you are lying on. I'll ignore it for now, but remember, this is my space.

Fortunately, caution and mutual respect finally gave way to tolerance. This evolved over a period of months, and was a huge lesson for both of them to learn.

Several years after Yellow Feathers joined the family, we had another unexpected arrival. But this time, it was because of an even more tragic event.

As I said in the last chapter, my brother died suddenly and violently. This was horrible for my family.

But let me tell you a little bit more about my brother, first, before I get into that.

My brother, Kenny, had just moved to Kansas City from Sarasota, Florida in the fall of 2014. Getting reconnected to him was a high priority for me, as we'd had a falling out three years prior. But my wife had just had a hip replacement, and he didn't have a car...we had hopes in the New Year that we'd be able to get together.

It's hard for me to remember Kenny now, because of what's happened since. But back then, he had grounded optimism. He liked being back in the Midwest. He seemed to be making a fresh start, and I was hoping for the best for him.

Kenny was the youngest in the family. He was a joy to be around, he never met a stranger, and was full of life. He'd lived with me for a year when I was in Connecticut and we got very close then. Now, after our three-year estrangement, we were communicating again via text and phone calls.

I finally had a chance to see him in person in April. It was early evening, and I could see him across the courtyard as he stood in front of his apartment looking for me. For some reason, that really warmed my heart. I walked across the courtyard, and we embraced; all was forgiven and we both believed that brighter days lay ahead.

Unfortunately, he died just a few weeks later, slain in his bed in a one-room apartment. And his two loyal, friendly, and loving dogs witnessed it all. Then the poor things had to stay in that room with their fallen master until the police arrived -- a period of several hours.

Can you imagine their terror?

I was told that they cowered in horror, fear, and sorrow, and were found huddled in the corner of the small room. One of the officers, a pet owner, lay on the floor until the dogs slowly made their way over. He was able to comfort them and hold their shivering bodies until the canine officers were able to remove them from the scene. It was a very touching story, with all the trauma and intense situations police deal with on a regular basis I was very indebted and amazed by this act of kindness.

They took Kenny's dogs to the local animal shelter. Fortunately, it happened to be the Kansas City Pet Project, a no-kill facility.

This all happened in early May 2015. My sister, Liz, older brother, Sam, and I met in Kansas City to take care of final details. (We came from different parts of the country.) While we dealt with the shock of my brother's gruesome murder, we knew for a couple days the dogs would be safe and sound. As we drove around Kansas City taking care of final matters, each one of us would bring up different items related to the dogs. We were concerned about their fate, and yet we were amazed at how well Kenny had taken care of them, considering Kenny hadn't always done a good job taking care of himself.

We had many things to take care of surrounding Ken's death. But ever-present in the back of our mind was what were we going to do with the dogs? We all knew how important they'd been to him. As he'd had no children, they were more like his babies.

None of us wanted these dogs to go outside the family. We also did not want them staying in the shelter forever. Since one dog was older and the other was young and cute, we did not want them split up either. We also decided that my older brother Sam, now in his seventies, was not the best choice to take these pups back to his home near Chicago. He insisted Liz or I take them. But Liz had flown in from Dallas, and certainly couldn't bring them back on the plane with her.

So, it was down to me. I had driven three hours from Southwest Missouri to get to KC, and I had the car. But it wasn't that simple. As I thought at the time, I have a blind dog, a giant dog, and a mean cat. I'm not sure about this.

But in hindsight, my older brother's wisdom was spot-on. He insisted we had to take the dogs right away. His intuition led to a short but powerful discovery about me and man's best friend.

Two weeks before Kenny's death, I had been at his apartment, and I met the dogs. They seemed nice enough. They seemed loved and well cared for despite the cramped quarters. I am glad I had that moment with them, and of course with my brother Ken.

So, decision made by default, I now had to go pick up these two small pets. Having had that short time with them a couple weeks before made the visit easier. Perhaps the dogs would be able to remember my scent. Maybe they would recognize me with their powerful nostrils identifying some family DNA strain, for all I knew.

When I walked into the large, well-run shelter, the dogs were front and center. It was touching to see them together in that double cage. Sam, Liz, and I had agreed they would have to stay together, and it was good to know the shelter seemed to understand that as well. Back home, Denise and Jay agreed this was a good, humane move and were looking forward to their arrival.

I cautiously stuck my finger through the cage and they gradually came to life. Then I got their licks and their tails started wagging. I had hopes that this may work.

The vet at the shelter had looked them both over. He determined that the younger dog, Barney, was nine years old. (He acted like nine months!) He was in good shape, but obviously depressed. The older dog, Greta, was sixteen. Time had begun to take its toll on her. She had dental disease, bulbous tumors, a hernia, was overweight, and had cataracts.

I thought, Two blind dogs in my house. Are you kidding me? How could we say no, though?

Yet another expense for which I was not prepared for, but there was no turning back.

The plan was for us to take them in for about a month and then bring them to my sister Liz. She had committed to keeping them for the long haul. We not only wanted to honor our brother's memory, but we felt deep compassion for these innocent animals.

As I was driving back from Kansas City with the dogs laying comfortably in the back seat. I distinctly heard my brother's voice in my head say, Thank you, David. I have heard no other words before or since, and have to believe it fulfilled one of his final wishes.

So we took them in. It was a new adventure for us all. Did I happen to mention they were dachshunds? And dachshunds are reputed to be territorial, protective, and snappy.

Greta happened to be 16, which is about 112 in dog years. I thought, Here we go, four dogs and a cat in a three bedroom, 1600 square foot small cottage. One of the dogs is almost old as Yoda and another is completely blind.

The time had come to bring these two new travelers through our front door. We put Hushie in the back yard. We wanted to introduce Lottie first. It went off without a hitch. Next we introduced Barney to Hushie, and they hit it off, too.

Now the test. We had a 112-year-old female dachshund and a blind beagle Basset -- a hound that likes to smell everything to the extreme! Which, of course, included the rear end of a 112-year-old female dog! Not a good mix!

When that happened, Greta growled and snapped at Hushie. (Do you blame her?)

He was defenseless, and backed away. He had developed this maneuver after running into Yellow Feathers quite a few times, as Yellow would hiss and swat at him. Hushie ended up growling and snapping back at air, nowhere near the perpetrator. Having Hushie and Greta work out their differences was going to take a little time.

The new dogs bounded around their new backyard paradise. They marked it up and made themselves at home. Barney especially was in all his glory. He was like a puppy jumping here and there, tail wagging around-the-clock. He would run back and leap into my lap as if to say “thank you,” then back off to this new playground. He honestly reminded me of Kenny, with kind of a Peter Pan quality to him.

Later that night as we sat by the fire pit, Yellow Feathers came out from behind the bushes. Barney, sitting in my lap, took a flying leap over the fire and almost caught the cat. Feeling some trepidation, I thought again, Is this going to work out?

There was tremendous change going on. Day by day we saw progress as the dogs worked out their differences. And Greta and Barney won our hearts quickly, so we indulged them a bit, especially because of what they'd just gone through. For example, we'd never let Hushie or Lottie get on the furniture, but decided it would be okay for these mini pups.

Of course, Lottie saw this indulgence, and decided to join the newcomers on our big, shabby chic, cushy chair. But in light of the recent events, did it matter?

Stepping back, I could see all was well with their world. We could extend that healing and grace to our long term household residents as well.

There were still issues between Hushie and Greta, much less Barney and Yellow Feathers. (After Barney had tried to pounce on the cat, Yellow could not be found. The feline eventually surfaced, but kept his distance.) It seemed to be a bit harder for Hushie since he was top dog, but in his defense he could not see a thing. We made it a point to lavish our love on all the critters. I must admit Barney and Greta got a bit more attention those few weeks Hushie eventually "manned up" and showed great character in not throwing his weight around. By the middle of the second week together, they all came to tolerate one another. Boundaries and respect of differences had led to tolerance.

Different Is Okay

I watched these dogs work out their differences right when our country was dealing with a string of domestic altercations involving black men and white police officers. The tensions were at a heightened level, and everyone was on edge. In the Middle East, ISIS was escalating its attacks against most of mankind. It made me wonder often, is it possible in our world for everyone to get along? Probably not. Can it be better? Most definitely yes. Can we have an impact on our smaller circle of influence? Undoubtedly.

What are some of our takeaways from this story?

First, we are all souls, human and canine alike. We are also all unique. Every one of us is different, down to each finger or paw print.

Differences spawn suspicion. Then the "FUD factor" of fear, uncertainty, and doubt takes over. That's not the greatest soil for spawning harmony and acceptance.

What can we all gather from this? Observing these dogs over time clued me in that they were acutely aware of their differences. There is nothing wrong with that. But they did not react in a defensive way. Instead, they acknowledged and accepted their differences.

Find Common Ground

Next, like the animals, we need to find our similarities and rally around that. The animals all had the similar goal to capture their master's attention. Each one from time to time would come for love and acceptance in the midst of this wave of change.

Every situation is different, but isn't it wise to find some common ground? Common ground fosters mutual respect. And mutual respect helped them tolerate each other's differences.

How can we acknowledge our differences, find common ground, and start to get along? Rodney King's cry is still relevant today. You may have discord in the family, or issues with in-laws. Perhaps there is strain with the neighbors, or suspicion with your coworker's motives.

My advice is to do one, simple thing: Stop. Step back, get and give a little space, and gain some perspective. That should allow mutual respect to blossom. Take that breath to allow for the capacity to tolerate differences.

We saw the animals do that. So why can't humans do the same thing?

I do need to point out one thing, though. In the case of my late brother's two dogs, when we brought them into our family, although indulged we created clear boundaries. They still had to interact and learn to get along. I think the boundaries helped our family adjust to Greta and Barney, and I think it also helped Greta and Barney adjust to us.

There's a lesson in that.

Boundaries Can Help

We all come from different places in life. We each have experiences that have shaped our lives. We come from unique customs and cultures. We have diverse lenses that shape our viewpoints. We have unique genetic wiring. All of that needs to be taken into account, but the simple, folk adage of "Good fences make good neighbors" may help, as it is full of wisdom.

To sum up, we took to heart the principles listed above and capitalized on them. We established clear boundaries. The dogs and cat were able to live in what was, at first, a testy environment. We humans should take note of that.

I mean, they had to share the same space-- and so do we.

The dogs ironed out their differences and eventually got along enough to tolerate one another on our small porch. We also received a bonus blessing. It came as a surprise!

Enjoy Moments Of Serendipity

Our goal with Barney and Greta was to take them in, keep them together, and help with their healing. But from the moment I picked them up from the shelter, these dogs brought an amazing power of healing into to my life. I had the opportunity to hold both dogs in my lap and let them lick my face. I was able to hug them tight. We even allowed them to sleep in our beds because of the trauma they'd been through. It was very cathartic to have them with us. I thought that we were here to help them, but they also helped me to process my grief.

All of it brought peace and healing in a deep and profound way. They seemed to now be at peace as well.

Chapter 7

Today Is My Last Day

Thoughts from Hushie:

I will never forget that trip to Columbia. Time slowed down. My muscles and senses all froze. When I saw my pack leader come to my cage at the hospital, I knew everything would be okay. He was the alpha male of our tribe. Well, I let him think he was. The hospital stay was one of those life events that required my complete trust. For six years he had never let me down I had no reason to believe this would be different.

Going back to the early days, my master seemed to fuss so much over my tail. I had no frame of reference to understand his anxiety. My concern was the way the humans would primp. I could never understand why they would put clothes on. I was always happy, though, when some ended up in a pile on the floor. I would circle around it, lay down on it and enjoy the pleasant scent. They would come along and interrupt my rapturous rest and take the cloth and put it in a pile in the laundry room.

But that didn't bother me too much, because that room was one of my favorite places to lie down. I could just plop down on my cloud-like cushion of familiar scents. It was always an aromatic feast, but always short-lived as I would get shooed away from that oasis.

The human pack was quite strange, but so loveable. They always scurried about. They fretted and worried. They sweated in their work. They believed themselves to be so evolved. They had many gadgets. They enjoyed moving images on a screen instead of going out and moving themselves. They knew how to make a living, but did they know how to live? I often wondered.

Still, I trust that some of my experience rubbed off on them. Once in a while, I got glimpses that they understood.

My favorite time was playing fetch in the backyard with my pack leaders. I loved to see the smile on their faces and hear the encouraging tones in their voices during those wonderful moments.

I was so grateful for my strong sense of smell. It served me well. You cannot imagine the intensity and the ways that I utilized it. I deciphered moods in humans. I tracked the pesky rabbit in the backyard. It helped me remember where I hid my dog bone. Even though blind, it always helped me find the ball when playing fetch.

Losing my sight was inconvenient, but it was not the end of my life. I had my sense of smell, my ability to move, my land, and my tribe. For my kind, it has always been all about the pack. Family was the word I often heard in our home. My most fulfilling times were when we would all lie on the ground together, hugging, petting, and licking one another. (Well, for some strange reason I was the only one who licked. Humans are so strange in their ways!)

All three humans could be completely trusted, they were firm, attentive, playful, dependable, and always fed me on time; earning the title of Pack Leaders over and over again.

As for my fellow travelers, I readily admit that my life was so enriched when Lottie came on the scene. She became my best buddy. (The cat, Yellow Feathers, not so much.) We made it work, though.

What a blessed life!

Then, Barney and Greta came into our home with no warning. It was a jolt to my world. There were only a few times when I was disappointed with my pack leader, but this was one of them. Lucky for all, it was short-lived. I liked having other dogs around, but the fat, little old dachshund just rubbed me the wrong way. We did learn to get along in pretty short order, though. Then they were gone as quickly as they arrived.

What can I say about those crazy humans and their impulses? Something was here today and gone tomorrow. Got to love them, though.

The summer after the dachshunds left brought some final challenges.

One hot summer day, we all crowded into the car. It reminded me of the days when I stood tall as the captain of this moving ship on wheels. Back then my rear paws were on the back seat and my front paws held me high to see out the front window. I stood on the middle arm rest and watched all the sights along the way. This day we stopped at this beautiful camp spot on the end of a road right on the lakefront. The sounds and smells were intoxicating. My master was so excited to have the whole family with him.

Then something odd hit me like a sledgehammer. I was waiting by the camp site in the hot sun, and I could feel my body seize up. (This had happened once before, a couple days prior, and it was one of the reasons my master wanted us all together. He wanted to keep an eye on me.) This episode was severe.

I remember that they walked me over into the shade before I collapsed onto my side. My legs stuck straight out, stiff and cramped. My body shook. My jaw opened as if someone was prying open an oyster shell. Then it locked open wide as I gasped for breath, and as I gurgled in my throat a horrible white foam came from my mouth.

A crowd gathered. One child gave my master a bottle of water. He cupped it in his hand and spoon-fed me as he did years ago. I sensed fear and compassion from all the humans.

After a half an hour, the attack stopped. I was dazed and confused. We packed up and went back home. Another trip to the vet was in order.

I heard my master say I was like a cat with nine lives. How could he say such a thing? It turns out that I now had Cushing's disease.

Things improved with my new medication, but I sensed my time on this planet might be winding down. I began to lose control of my bladder all the time. I would wake up Ms. Master three to four times a night. (My male master slept with his nice, soft rolling snore filling the air. He was oblivious to our night time routine.)

I felt like our time together was coming to an end. There was more frustration and sadness in the house. I was petted more. My tribe got down on the floor with me a bit more. My eyes had failed long ago, but now my muscles, my nerves, and my bladder were breaking down, too.

Worst of all, my appetite started to wane. One day, my pack leader placed a ribeye steak in front of me. The whole steak. I had never smelled such splendor. I thought, Why now? Why did you wait to indulge me with this epicurean delight at this point in my life? I could not finish it. But it gave me hope for my future. What other surprises might yet await me?

It was a sunny spring day and I still felt a bit frisky. I played fetch twice that day and found the ball every time. I was not used to that much of a workout. At three in the morning, I began to go into one of my seizures. Jay woke up and tried to comfort me. Soon the alpha master came and moved me free from Jay's door. I went through a series of five seizures in an hour. I was limp and barely conscious, but I felt it as Jay and my alpha master lifted me into the truck. Like all the times before I thought, I know my master will help me and make me feel better.

But somehow, I sensed this trip was different. I was still panting and felt extremely hot. My master and I had developed such a deep, strong bond over the years, and I could sense the great sadness in his spirit.

While it was still dark, we got to the vet, an all-too-familiar place. I was not panicky, as I had been in my younger days. Time and again, I'd come in, and walked away feeling better than when I arrived. Wouldn't this be the same?

I could not stand, so they put me on a rolling table and strapped me down. My master got on the ground with me and hugged my neck. How strange, as we were right in the middle of the clinic. I felt both proud and embarrassed at the same time. I felt loved.

He put his face on mine. I sniffed and felt the salt water coming down from his eyes. This was different. Although I was in pain I thought, Is there a new home I am going to? Will it also be full of love and laughter?

The vet's assistants pried my master's hands from around me. I had a strange sense of peace and finality. I believed, somehow, that better days will be ahead for both of us.

As we parted, I sensed a deep, soulful stare from my master. My sixth sense realized he was holding onto overwhelming heartache. I nuzzled my dry nose on his face. We snuggled one last time. We were connected, deep and true. Although I couldn't show it any more, I felt my tail wag inside me one last time.

But it was not noticeable to my master. I sensed that more tears streamed down his face, but I also had the impression there was a smile, too. He then told me, "Thank you, Hushie."

I felt complete.

I knew, now, that today was my last day. I felt special and privileged to share my life so deeply with another being. Now I prayed my own serenity prayer and released myself back to our Maker. It was well.

All was well with my soul.

Final Thoughts

I walked through the door of the vet clinic without my beloved friend Hushie. I was overcome with a sense of loss only a pet owner can know. Sometimes, even when we know the end is coming, it can come out of nowhere. This was not how I'd planned it. I was deeply sad and felt blindsided.

Overnight, Hushie's temperature had risen to 107 degrees. He had been suffering, and in pain. The vets confirmed there was brain damage and he would not be able to function. I had to make the decision to euthanize him.

Although Denise and I had talked about it before, I did not realize it would all happen so suddenly. Earlier, I'd texted both Jay and Denise that the news was not good. Once the decision was made, the vets said Hushie would be out of his pain in a couple of minutes. I called Jay and told him the news and we just both cried on the phone.

As the days slowly rolled by, I would see Hushie in my mind's eye all around our home. Set times of the day were dedicated to him; so many memories were evoked. I cried many tears and came to realize they were the lubricant for healing my heart.

Yet I had so many questions. We were given twelve years with this delightful pet. Why is there only a ten to fifteen year life span for these wonderful animals? Why do we put ourselves in this situation knowing we only have a few years, and that this would be the end result? Why aren't these most beloved animals spoken more highly in Scripture? Do all dogs really go to heaven?

I don't know the answers. I do know the depth and riches of this wonderful connection.

A week after Hushie died, we drove home with his ashes, but couldn't make it all the way without breaking down. Instead, I pulled off to the side of the road and wept like a baby. It was a sunny, cold early spring day, but I felt a strange warmth and peace come over me.

I arrived home and opened the fence to Hushie's kingdom. The same shadows again fell across the landscape that he'd ruled for years. I walked toward the shed that housed the rabbits he stalked daily. Lottie walked beside me. She sniffed the ashes and hung her tail low.

The family gathered together. Deliberately, I spread the ashes around the perimeter of the shed, as I was sure that's what Hushie would've wanted. It would be one last stand by our persistent pooch.

Then, for some reason, I imagined Hushie now romping on a rolling hillside, enjoying the rabbits all around him. He finally caught one, and they frolicked and played like school kids at recess. I visualized him later playing fetch with an automatic ball machine. That ribeye steak he'd eaten as one of his last meals was now an everyday staple for him. And I saw a pack with a human, dog, and cat together playing, snuggling, and sleeping happily ever after.

I saw that .... My blind dog could now see.

Author's Afterword

Unconditional love and companionship are perhaps the most common qualities dog owners attribute to their dear pets. I have seen and experienced it with my cherished four-legged friends, most particularly Hushie.

Dogs are always there for us. They love to see us, and greet us. They love to please us. Always! They see and know everything about us – the good, and the not-so-good. Despite that, they still want to climb in our laps and cuddle up.

It is a great energizer to know that someone sees the real you and still loves you, no matter what.

Dogs don't talk back or criticize. These collective qualities alone are more than enough to fulfill a deep need in our lives. It helps to forge a union that is real and true.

If we look closely, we can observe many other qualities from our pets that enlighten and enrich our lives. They can learn from us, and we certainly can learn from them. They are a wonderful gift.

Take time today to give a scratch behind the ears, a sweet nuzzle and a pat on the back to all those in your home, pets and human alike.

I want to thank all of my critters for the gift of healing and love that they have brought me. I will pass on the lessons and principles described in this book. I will continue to be open to new lessons from my best friends. I will try to slow down and make my life a bit simpler and give to others a bit more. I will not only stop and smell the roses, but an occasional paw. The simplest truths, after all, are sometimes the greatest, aren't they?

In the end I trust that our beloved Hushie and his fellow canine crew of Lottie, Greta, and Barney are better off for my love and attention. (I will even include Yellow Feathers in that tribe.) I know I am better off because of the relationship I had with my dear furry, funny critter companion Hushie, and I'll never forget him.

To all best friends everywhere, pass the love on.

Appendix

Appendix

No Kill Animal Shelters in the U.S.

www.nokillnetwork.org/no-kill-animal-shelters.php

www.kcpetproject.org

www.carerescue.org

www.bestfriends.org/Resources/No-Kill-Resources

Service Dogs & Agency Links

www.4pawsforability.org

4 Paws for Ability enriches the lives of children with disabilities by training and placing quality, task-trained service dogs. This provides increased independence for the children, and assistance to their families. And 4 Paws also works with veterans from recent conflicts who've lost the use of their limbs or their hearing while in active combat. In all cases, the results speak for themselves.

www.akc.org

Since the 1980's, there have been significant advances in the field of animal assisted therapy and the use of therapy dogs. Organized therapy dog groups provide educational material to volunteers, they screen both volunteers and dogs, and they provide liability insurance for when the dog and handler are volunteering in a therapy setting. Follow this link to multiple resources for therapy dogs via the American Kennel Club.

www.assistancedogsinternational.org

Assistance Dogs International (ADI) is a coalition of not for profit assistance dog organizations. The purpose of ADI is to improve the areas of training, placement, and utilization of assistance dogs, staff and volunteer education, as well as educating the public about assistance dogs, and advocating for the legal rights of people with disabilities partnered with assistancedogs.

www.k9s4cops.org/kids

A safe learning environment is a basic requirement for educators and students alike. Safety features and plans are being reevaluated and discussions are being held on how to best to provide more security. K9s4KIDs was launched from these discussions with the initiative to reach out to school district and college campus police and offer K9s trained and ready for action.

www.pawswithacause.org

Paws With A Cause enhances the independence and quality of life for people with disabilities nationally through custom trained Assistance Dogs. PAWS increases awareness of the rights and roles of Assistance Dog Teams through education and advocacy.

www.petpartners.org

Pet Partners is the national leader in demonstrating and promoting positive human-animal therapy, activities and education. Nearly forty years since the organization's inception, the science that proves these benefits has become indisputable. Today, Pet Partners is the nation's largest and most prestigious nonprofit registering handlers of multiple species as volunteer teams providing animal-assisted interactions.

www.seeingeye.org

Since 1929 the Seeing Eye's mission is to enhance the independence, dignity and self-confidence of people who are blind, through the use of specially trained Seeing Eye® dogs.

In pursuit of this mission, The Seeing Eye breeds and raises puppies to become Seeing Eye dogs, trains Seeing Eye dogs to guide blind people, instructs blind people in the proper use, handling, and care of the dogs and conducts and supports research on canine health and development.

www.tdi-dog.org/Default.aspx

Therapy Dogs International (TDI®) is a volunteer organization dedicated to regulating, testing and registration of therapy dogs and their volunteer handlers for the purpose of visiting nursing homes, hospitals, other institutions and wherever else therapy dogs are needed.

www.eterantraveler.com/service-dog-agencies

An inspiring site devoted to dogs and the vets they support. Many resources, blogs, links and stories of real heroes – canine and human.

Dog Fun Facts – related to Hushie stories

Dog Senses

***Credit* – www.vetinfo.com/canine-vision.html**

How Your Dog Sees the World

Your dog sees the world from about one to two feet off the ground. Canine vision has evolved to fit their conditions and lifestyle. Typically, dogs judge an object in three different ways. The first is motion, the second is contrast (a dark figure against a white background), and the third is color.

Superior Sense of Motion

A canine's sense of motion is far superior to a human's ability. Perhaps this is one of the reasons why many dogs don't show interest in television, as instead of seeing fluid moving pictures, the dog sees flashes of light. That is, the many individual flashes of a single picture on a film strip that create the fluid motion we perceive. In fact, a dog's determination of motion is so good, it can see a moving object more than half a mile away. However, if that item is stationary, a dog can only determine that an object is there if it's 600 yards away.

Visual Acuity

The average dog has 20/75 vision, meaning a dog sees the same thing at 20 ft. that a human with normal vision can see at 75 ft. Also, objects closer than 33 cm. to their eyes appear blurry to dogs. Compare that to a human with perfect vision who can still see the details of an object only 7 cm. away from their eyes.

Field of Vision Correlates with Nose

The range of vision a dog can see is relevant to the breed and how close together his eyes are. As a rule of thumb, the longer a dog's nose, the greater his field of vision (the more he can see in his peripheral vision). A human's total view is about 180 degrees. A Pug or Pekinese dog has a field of vision that is 220 degrees, while a long-nosed Afghan Hound or Borzoi has a 290 degree field of vision.

Limited Color Perception

Like human eyes, canine eyes consist of cones and rods; however, there is an emphasis on their rods, while we have an emphasis on cones. Their emphasis allows them to see in the dark and dim light four times better than we can. The emphasis on human cones allows us to have a greater spectrum of colors in bright light. We have three cones, while dogs have only two. Contrary to popular belief, they are not color blind, but able to determine various shades of violet, indigo, and blue, and possibly red. They have difficulty distinguishing colors between green, yellow, orange and red. The color blue-green appears white or a shade of gray to them. Though our canine companions seem to have less ability determining colors, they are actually much better at differentiating subtler shades of gray than humans are.

The Difference Between Human and Canine Vision

Credit - www.FindRetrievers.com

Dog vision is pretty different from ours. The human and canine eye are built much the same, but each has modifications that make it suit the individual specie's lifestyle. Humans evolved as a diurnal species (active in daytime) and canines evolved as a nocturnal species (active at dawn and dusk). As a result the human has less ability to see in low light conditions but has better visual acuity, which is the ability to focus so that two objects appear as distinct entities.

A human with 20/20 vision has excellent visual acuity. A typical dog has 20/75 vision which means their vision is 6 times poorer than ours. A dog must stand 20 feet away from an object that a human can see at 75 feet. The dog has to get much closer to the object than a human. This is due to the fact that dogs have fewer cones in their retinas than people. Cones handle color and daytime vision, and rods handle night time vision.

These are the two types of specialized receptors in our eyes, rods and cones. Rods are dominant in the retinas of nocturnal animals, and cones are dominant in the retinas of diurnal animals. In animals where fine vision is critical such as humans, a small pure cone area called the fovea is placed directly in the center of your line of vision. The fovea is the part of your eye that you are using to read this text and covers just a small area of your vision. Now try reading with your finger blocking your central vision and notice how difficult it is. This can give you some idea of how it must be like for an animal without a fovea to make out fine detail.

There is also much variation in visual acuity among the different breeds of dogs, as well as among individuals of a breed. You've probably seen bulls in bullfights lower their heads before they charge the matador. Border collies do the same thing when they're herding sheep. They lower their heads below their shoulders and stare at the sheep. They do this because their retinas are different from ours. Domestic animals have a *visual streak* instead of a human fovea. The visual streak is a straight line across the back of the retina. When you see an animal lower its head to look

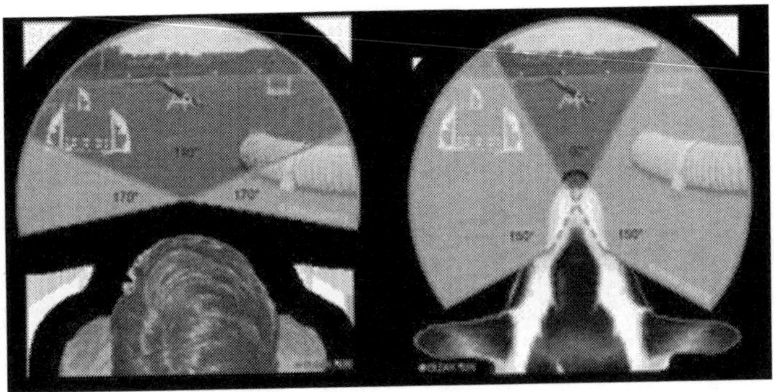

at something, it's probably getting the image lined up on its visual streak. Researchers also have found the two fastest animals, the cheetah and the greyhound, to have the most highly developed visual streaks which are dense with photoreceptors, giving them extra-acute vision.

Another huge difference between humans and canines is that canines have panoramic vision. The position of the eyes within the head determines the degree of peripheral vision as well as the amount of the visual field that is seen simultaneously with both eyes. This binocular vision is necessary for judgment of distances. Dogs have eyes which are placed on the sides of the head, resulting in a visual field of 240 degrees compared with the human field of 200 degrees. The central, binocular field of vision in dogs is approximately half that possessed by humans.

The third area where humans and canines differ is the ability to see color and contrast. The perception of color is determined by the presence of cone photoreceptors within the retina. These cone cells function in bright light conditions and comprise approximately 20% of the photoreceptors in the central retina of the dog. In humans, the central retina (macula) is 100% cones. Animals see more intense contrasts of light and dark because their night vision is so much better than ours. Good night vision involves excellent vision for contrasts and relatively poor color vision.

You need to know something about an animals' color vision to predict what visual stimuli they'll experience as high-contrast. Birds see four different basic colors (ultraviolet,

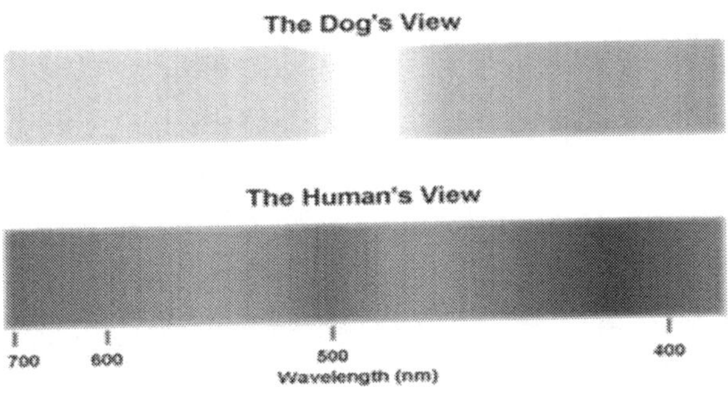

blue, green and red), people and some primates see three (blue, green, red), and most of the rest of the mammals just see two (blue and green). With dichromatic, or two-color, vision the colors the animal sees best are a yellowish green (the color of a safety vest) and bluish purple. That means yellow is the high-contrast color for almost all animals.

Other Dog Senses reference links:

www.dog-vision.com/#Color

This site provides a web based image processing tool that can be used to demonstrate the differences in visual perception between humans and dogs.

www.dogbreedinfo.com/articles/dogsenses.htm

A big part of understanding your dog is understanding its senses and accepting that they are indeed different than humans. Both humans and dogs have the same three senses: sight, hearing and smelling, however while most humans communicate by hearing, seeing, and then smelling, dogs primarily communicate by smelling, seeing and lastly hearing. Dogs also have a universal sense which humans do not have, where they can feel the energy (emotions) of the other beings around them.

Quotes about Dogs

"No man can be condemned for owning a dog. As long as he has a dog, he has a friend." —**Will Rogers**

"Happiness is a warm puppy." —**Charles M. Schulz**

"The average dog is a nicer person than the average person." —**Andy Rooney**

"If a dog will not come to you having looked you in the face, you should go home and examine your conscience." —**Woodrow Wilson**

"The dog was created especially for children. He is the-god of frolic." —**Henry Ward Beecher**

"Buy a pup and your money will buy love unflinching." —**Rudyard Kipling**

"A person can learn a lot from a dog, even a loopy one like ours. Marley taught me about living each day with unbridled exuberance and joy, about seizing the moment and following your heart. He taught me to appreciate the simple things - a walk in the woods, a fresh snowfall, a nap in a shaft of winter sunlight. And as he grew old and achy, he taught me about optimism in the face of adversity. Mostly, he taught me about friendship and selflessness and, above all else, unwavering loyalty." —**Josh Grogan**

"The better I get to know men, the more I find myself loving dogs." —**Charles de Gaulle**

"When you have dogs, you witness their uncomplaining acceptance of suffering, their bright desire to make the most of life in spite of the limitations of age and disease, their calm awareness of the approaching end when their final hours come. They accept death with a grace that I hope I will one day be brave enough to muster."
—**Dean Koontz**

"To his dog, every man is Napoleon; hence the constant popularity of dogs." —**Aldous Huxley**

"Dogs have given us their absolute all. We are the center of their universe. We are the focus of their love and faith and trust. They serve us in return for scraps. It is without a doubt the best deal man has ever made." —**Roger A. Caras**

"I'm suspicious of people who don't like dogs, but I trust a dog when it doesn't like a person." —**Bill Murray**

"I think dogs are the most amazing creatures. They give unconditional love. For me they are a role model for being alive." —**Gilda Radner**

"Heaven goes by favor. If it went by merit, you would stay out and your dog would go in." —**Mark Twain**

"I've seen a look in a dog's eyes, a quickly vanishing look of amazed contempt, and I am convinced that dogs think we humans are nuts." —**John Steinbeck**

"I care not for a man's religion whose dog and cat are not the better for it." —**Abraham Lincoln**

"Every dog must have his day." —**Jonathan Swift**

"Dogs are minor angels, and I don't mean that facetiously. They love unconditionally, forgive immediately, are the truest of friends, willing to do anything that makes us happy, etcetera. If we attributed some of those qualities to a person we would say they are special. If they had ALL of them, we would call them angelic. But because it's 'only' a dog, we dismiss them as sweet or funny but little more. However, when you think about it, what are the things that we most like in another human being? Many times those qualities are seen in our dogs every single day-- we're just so used to them that we pay no attention." —**Jonathan Carrol**

"The dog is the most faithful of animals and would be much esteemed were it not so common. Our Lord God has made His greatest gifts the commonest." — **Martin Luther**

"The dog's agenda is simple, fathomable, overt: I want. "I want to go out, come in, eat something, lie here, play with that, kiss you.There are no ulterior motives with a dog, no mind games, no second- guessing, no complicated negotiations or bargains, and no guilt trips or grudges if a request is denied." —**Caroline Knapp**

"If a man aspires to a righteous life, his first act of abstinence is from injury to animals." —**Albert Einstein**

"Dogs' lives are short, too short, but you know that going in. You know the pain is coming, you're going to lose a dog, and there's going to be great anguish, so you live fully in the moment with her, never fail to share her joy or delight in her innocence, because you can't support the illusion that a dog can be your lifelong companion. There's such beauty in the hard honesty of that, in accepting and giving love while always aware that it comes with an unbearable price. Maybe loving dogs is a way we do penance for all the other illusions we allow ourselves and the mistakes we make because of those illusions."
—**Dean Koontz**

"A lot of shelter dogs are mutts like me." —**Barack Obama**

"You want a friend in this city? [Washington, DC.] Get a dog!" —**Harry S. Truman**

"In his grief over the loss of a dog, a little boy stands for the first time on tiptoe, peering into the rueful morrow of manhood. After this most inconsolable of sorrows there is nothing life can do to him that he will not be able somehow to bear." —**James Thurber**

"The poor dog. In life the firmest friend. The first to welcome. Foremost to defend." —**Lord Byron**

"A dog teaches a boy fidelity, perseverance, and to turn around three times before lying down." —**Robert Benchley**

"Petting, scratching, and cuddling a dog could be as soothing to the mind and heart as deep meditation and almost as good for the soul as prayer." —**Dean Koontz**

Growth Resources

inspirational, motivational, and instructional links from those referenced in the book

www.joniandfriends.org/jonis-corner/jonis-bio/

Joni Eareckson Tada, the Founder and CEO of Joni and Friends International Disability Center, is an international advocate for people with disabilities. A diving accident in 1967 left Joni Eareckson, then 17, a quadriplegic in a wheelchair, without the use of her hands. After two years of rehabilitation, she emerged with new skills and fresh determination to help others in similar situations.

www.jimabbott.net/biography.html?submenuheader=0

Jim Abbott was born September 19, 1967, in Flint, Michigan without a right hand. He was an All-America hurler at Michigan; won the Sullivan Award in 1987; was the pitcher for the Gold Medal Olympic Team in 1988; and threw a 4-0 no-hitter for the New York Yankees versus Cleveland (September 4, 1993). Jim played for 10 seasons on 4 different teams and ended his big league playing career in 1999. Abbott has worked with The Department of Labor's Office of Disability Employment Policy (ODEP) on several initiatives encouraging businesses to hire peoplewithdisabilities. Today, in addition to often being a Guest Pitching Instructor during Spring Training for the Los Angeles Angels, Jim Abbott is a motivational speaker.

www.imdb.com/title/tt0440382/

In its sum, it was a postseason that begged the question, "Can you believe it?"

Against all odds, the ***2004 Red Sox*** would become the first major league team to rally from a 3-0 deficit in a seven-game series, beating the Yankees in an epic American League Championship Series on their way to their first World Series title since 1918.

Ten years later, **ESPNBoston.com** looks back to determine the moment from that magical run that stands out the most.

Motivated Gifts & Behavior Resources

www.arthurfmiller.com/

Each person arrives on earth possessing an inborn behavior pattern, which has a five-part structure, certain content and behavioral dynamics. Each pattern and employee is unique in coded detail. Containing 15-25 elements of behavior, occasionally more. Composed of abilities, subjects matter, circumstances, relationships, and an outcome the employee is determined to achieve. This pattern triggers, sustains, and governs motivated behavior

www.simainternational.com/powered-by-sima/

The System for Identifying Motivated Abilities® (SIMA®) is a proprietary, non- psychological, qualitative process for clearly identifying a person's *innate giftedness*—their motivated strengths, interests, contextual circumstances, preferred roles, and motivational drives.

Using SIMA®, we can demonstrate that every person has been endowed with a uniquely motivated and purposeful behavioral pattern. When people live and work in accordance with their pattern, they experience remarkably productive and meaningful lives.

www.mycallingiq.com/giftedness-or-motivated-abilities-pattern-exercise/

"Giftedness is the way we are by nature. It's what makes us us. It's the way we were designed to function, and therefore the way we actually do function best and with the greatest delight. It includes what we do well and are motivated to accomplish." "Giftedness is not limited to school smarts, genius-level intelligence or precocious musical talent, it is not a personality type or trait and it is not some quality that can be acquired." "Because it is like breathing, every person has used their giftedness throughout their years, be those years long or short."

www.truecolorsintl.com/

Established in 1978 and servicing a multitude of countries worldwide, translated into over 16 languages and with more than 6,000 registered trainers, True Colors has stood the test of time.

When compared to other personality assessment tools True Colors has been repeatedly found to supersede all competition. It is easy to use, it is easy to remember and it is proven to have great beneficial effects for any group that applies it.

The 'Language' of the colors and the 'AHA!' moment can be reached within a few minutes from the introduction to True Colors. People of all ages and walks of life are able to embrace this simple language that encapsulates the complex nature of personalities; Orange, Gold, Green and Blue.

Fast, memorable, valid and useful, an introduction to True Colors is the valuable gift of insights for life.

Like Us on Facebook
"J.D. Wilcock" and also
"My Blind Dog Still Wags His Tail"

Above all -

For God so loved the world
that He gave his one and only Son,
that whoever believes in Him will not perish,
but will have eternal life
John 3:16 NIV

40018290R00078

Made in the USA
San Bernardino, CA
09 October 2016